synago

Calm in the Storm

By Karen Kluever

Senior High
Student-Led
Small Groups

Calm in the Storm

Student-Led Senior High Small Groups

A small group ministry resource for reaching, nurturing, encouraging, and discipling senior high youth

by Karen Kluever

Scripture Credits

Contemporary English Version (CEV)
Scripture quotations marked (CEV) are from the Contemporary English Version copyright © 1991, 1992, 1995 by American Bible Society. Used by permission.

The Message (Message)
Scripture taken from THE MESSAGE. Copyright © Eugene H. Peterson, 1993, 1994, 1995. Used by permission of NavPress Publishing Group.

New Century Version (NCV)
Scriptures quoted from The Holy Bible, New Century Version, copyright © 1987, 1988, 1991 by Word Publishing, Nashville, Tennessee 37214. Used by permission.

New International Version (NIV)
Scripture quotations marked (NIV) are taken from the HOLY BIBLE, NEW INTERNATIONAL VERSION® NIV®. Copyright © 1973, 1978, 1984 by International Bible Society. Used by permission of Zondervan Publishing House. All rights reserved.

New Revised Standard Version (NRSV)
New Revised Standard Version of the Bible, copyright 1989, Divisions of Christian Education of the National Council of Churches of Christ in the United States of America. Used by permission. All rights reserved.

About the Author

Karen Kluever has a heart for teenagers. She is currently in ministry with youth at Mouzon United Methodist Church, in Charlotte, North Carolina, where she serves as director of program ministries. *Synago* comes from her experience with youth at Myers Park United Methodist, also in Charlotte, where she served as youth program coordinator for eleven years. Karen loves developing resources for youth and was the editorial assistant for *The Magazine for Christian Youth!* before moving to North Carolina. She has also written curriculum for middle school youth.

Karen has undergraduate and graduate degrees in journalism and a master's in Christian education from Pfeiffer University, in North Carolina. She is married and has three sons, ages 8, 11, and 13. (Karen says that she thinks it's great to finally have two of her own kids in youth ministry with her.)

> "I no longer call you servants. . . . Instead, I have called you friends, for everything that I learned from my Father I have made known to you. You did not choose me, but I chose you and appointed you to go and bear fruit—fruit that will last. . . . This is my command: Love each other."
> —Jesus
> (John 15:15-17, NIV)

03 04 05 06 07 08 09 10 11—10 9 8 7 6 5 4 3 2

What's Synago?

Synago (syn-AH-go) is the Greek word for "come together."
You may recognize it as the root word of *synagogue,* a place
were people come together to worship and to learn the faith.
And so it is with these student-led small groups. Youth
come seeking God, wanting to learn.

Synago can also be translated "to take in." One of the
purposes of these student-led small groups is to reach out
and invite in youth who have not been a part of a church,
youth who do not have a relationship with God through
Jesus Christ, youth who are seeking or perhaps struggling
with faith. Friends invite
friends, and the group takes
them in with love.

Synago is also the root word
of *synergy,* where the coming
together of individual parts
makes something even
greater. And so it is in these
small groups. In coming
together to talk about their
lives in light of God's good
news, the group members
find that something great
happens.

Contents

From the Author

This resource came about, as many do, out of necessity.

While I was serving on the youth ministries staff of a large, urban church, we began to have this gnawing, restless feeling that our youth program—although "successful" in terms of variety and quality of offerings and numbers of active youth—was not successful in the way we felt it should be. We wanted to see more youth in Bible studies, mentoring relationships, and leadership roles. We wanted to see that, in addition to their participation, our youth were actually maturing in faith, growing as disciples of Jesus Christ, and living out their faith commitment in their daily lives. We wanted more than "numbers" success; we wanted "depth" success.

Convinced that small groups could provide ideal opportunities and environments for inviting, discipling, and nurturing youth in the Christian faith, we took several stabs at small group ministry over the years. We offered adult-led Bible study at church during the week; adult-led Bible study in homes during the week; and adult-led topical studies once a month at Sunday night youth group, where students were assigned to different groups to encourage building new relationships. These strategies didn't deliver — for our youth group, anyway — what we wanted them to. To paraphrase what one inventor said, We didn't make mistakes, we just learned how not to do it.

Because the small group bug was still biting, I attended a seminar on student-led cell groups. As the seminar leader described the cell group philosophy and design for student-led small groups, I knew I was close to hitting pay dirt. What sold me was the personal story-sharing of a student cell group leader. When she spoke of "ministering" to members of her cell group, in the sense of caring for them and encouraging them in the love of Christ, I imagined those same words and the passion with which they were spoken coming from my students back home.

> We wanted more than "numbers" success; we wanted "depth" success.

A team of student and adult leaders in our youth program was formed to pray about and to consider a new design for small group ministry. We checked out several models and resources. In true youth ministry fashion, we took some of this, some of that, and tossed in some of our own stuff, resulting in the design and suggestions I share with you in this resource. In developing our own format for student-led small groups, however, we "designed ourselves out" of finding curriculum that worked with our model. During our first year of student-led small groups, I modified available curriculum to fit our needs.

We felt successful with our first year's attempt. We had started the academic year with four groups and ended with eight; student leaders had stepped up to the leadership task and excelled; group members were inviting their friends (both church members and non church members); commitment to attending the weekly meetings was extremely high; our student leaders and adult counselors were enthusiastic; and we also experienced a significant increase in the number of senior high youth participating in Sunday night youth fellowship, retreats, mission trips, and so on.

In gearing up for a second year of student-led small groups, we were once again in need of a topical, Bible study resource designed for our situation. So, inspired and guided by the Spirit, with deep love and compassion for "my kids" at Myers Park Church and their friends, and out of pure necessity—the first two volumes of this curriculum for student-led senior high small groups were created. I hope that you will make it your own, using it in whatever way the Spirit leads you. Blessings!

—Karen Kluever

Jesus said it. . . .

"For where two or three are gathered in my name, I am there among them."
(Matthew 18:20, NRSV)

Jesus did it. . . .

He went up the mountain and called to him those whom he wanted, and they came to him. And he appointed twelve, whom he also named apostles, to be with him, and to be sent out to proclaim the message.
(Mark 3:13-14, NRSV)

So did the first Christians. . . .

All who believed were together and had all things in common. . . . Day by day, as they spent much time together in the temple, they broke bread at home and ate their food with glad and generous hearts, praising God and having the goodwill of all the people. And day by day the Lord added to their number those who were being saved.
(Acts 2:44, 46-47, NRSV)

And there is more. . . .

"If you continue in my word, you are truly my disciples; and you will know the truth, and the truth will make you free."
(John 8:31-32, NRSV)

Therefore confess your sins to one another, and pray for one another, so that you may be healed.
(James 5:16, NRSV)

We loved you so much that we were delighted to share with you not only the gospel of God but our lives as well, because you had become so dear to us.
(1 Thessalonians 2:8, NIV)

Getting Started

To the Ones in Charge

If you are...

___ in charge of   ___ responsible for   ___ interested in

the . . .

___ supervising   ___ coordinating   ___ "selling"   ___ start up

of a senior high small group ministry in your...

___ church   ___ community   ___ organization   ___ school

and whether you are...

___ a paid youth worker   ___ a volunteer youth worker

___ not sure why someone gave you this resource and said "Good luck"

you are definitely...

___ embarking on   ___ continuing on

an exciting, high-impact adventure in youth ministry. *Synago* offers guidelines and suggestions for beginning and implementing a senior high, student-led, small group ministry, as well as providing 16 sessions for your student leaders to use in their small groups. (That's good for a semester's worth of small group meetings.)

As the person . . .

___ in charge of   ___ "volunteered for"

providing leadership for this ministry, the first section of this resource is to help you start, coordinate, and supervise *Synago* small groups.

What's Synago All About?

First and foremost, the goal of the small group is to strengthen members' spiritual relationship with God and Jesus Christ.

The sessions are led by trained student leaders, who are committed to living out, growing in, and encouraging their peers in the Christian faith. These student leaders are nurtured, supported, and supervised by one or more Christian youth workers—the counselor who is a member of their small group and possibly a small group coordinator and/or a youth ministry director.

Small group sessions are designed to help youth connect their "story" with "the Story" of the Christian faith. They discuss where their own experience and understanding of a particular life or faith issue comes together with the Scripture. Then they consider how God's love, grace, forgiveness, and call to faithfulness can have an impact upon that area of their lives.

Sessions explore topics such as anxiety, gossip, prayer, family relationships, friends, suffering, service, dating, confrontation, self-esteem, setting goals, and lots more. Generally, each session is topically based and explores one or more Bible readings, which group members analyze, interpret, and then apply to their own lives.

The second purpose of the small group is to build Christian community within a circle of friends, in which group members practice and experience what it means to be in ministry to and with one another.

The small group is friendship based. Members are not assigned to a group, but invited to the group by the group leaders or other members. Invited friends may or may not be members of the church or organization sponsoring the small group ministry, which makes this ministry an excellent way to reach beyond the walls of the church to youth who are unchurched or currently inactive.

Synago groups usually meet in the homes of group members. Since one of the goals is to reach out especially to unchurched youth, having the meeting in homes can overcome the reluctance some youth may feel about coming to something at a church building.

To encourage intimacy and trust, a policy of honesty, openmindedness, and confidentiality is communicated at each session: "What is shared in the group, stays in the group." This policy frees students to talk about very personal and sometimes painful circumstances of their lives in a loving, compassionate, and supportive environment.

Each small group has two student leaders, an adult counselor (or couple) and up to seven other student members. When there is a consistent participation of ten members, the group "multiplies" into two groups. Typically, the original co-leaders each go to one of the new groups and begin leading with a new co-leader. Additional adult leadership is then assigned to one of the new groups. Recruitment and training for both student leaders and adult counselors should happen at least two times during the year, in order to have leadership available when it comes time for a group to multiply.

For more nuts and bolts info, check out pages 13 and 19.

Great Reasons for Student-Led Small Groups

1 Built-in Intimacy

group members already acquainted; care about one another

2 Greater Commitment to the Group

because it's led by friends; friends encourage one another's attendance

3 More Youth Than Youth Workers

to reach other youth both in and outside the church

4 Leadership Development

especially of the student leaders

5 Biblical Roots

the disciples and early Christian church

6 Youth Drawn to Christ Through Their Circle of Friends

by their love, care, encouragement, and support

How to Do Student-Led Small Groups

- Meet once a week.
- Meet in homes of group members (may stay at one location for 2–4 weeks).
- Meet for 1½ hours. The day and time is to be determined by co-leaders (who may have the input of group members).
- Have two student co-leaders.
- Have at least one adult counselor. (There may be two counselors.)
- Have a spiritual mix (see below).
- Maintain the group at a maximum of ten regular members. If the group grows beyond ten members, multiply into two groups.
- Grow by inviting friends.
- Use topical sessions with faith applications
- Maintain the group as a safe, confidential place to gather as a faith community.

Spiritual Mix

What is a spiritual mix? Each group should strive for a mix of members at different levels of faith maturity. By intentionally keeping the group open to all persons, the members help one another. Everyone brings something to the group; everyone gains something from the group.

Non-Christians and New Converts

Non-Christians and new converts need care and encouragement from the small group. With their searching questions and interest in learning about Christianity, these youth challenge the more mature Christians to reflect on and articulate their faith and spiritual experiences in a way that makes sense to others who do not share the same experiences or faith language.

Struggling Christians

Struggling Christians are those who have made a commitment to the Christian faith but who are dealing with one or more serious problems with family, school, friends, faith, and so forth. They also need care and encouragement from group members during a difficult time in their lives. The small group will be a safe place to talk about their problems and to receive God's care, support, and healing through the loving expressions of other group members.

Strong Christians

These students should be encouraged to continue growing in their faith and living it out in all the areas of their lives. They should be expected to accept specific leadership roles in the small group or in other ministries of the church. As they are faced with the needs and questions of group members with little or no Christian background, or who are struggling with issues in their lives, the stronger Christians will have opportunities to share God's love with friends and encourage them with their own faith stories.

Typical Format

15 minutes ┄┄→ Socializing
Don't forget the snacks.

5 minutes ┄┄→ Opening
Welcome new members.
Make announcements (such as upcoming youth group
and church activities).
Read Purpose Statement.
Pray together.

8 minutes ┄┄→ Warm-Up
Start the group thinking.

15 minutes ┄┄→ Topic Talk
Introduce and get into the topic.

15 minutes ┄┄→ Word Search
Read and examine the biblical text.

15 minutes ┄┄→ R & R—Reflect and Respond
Discuss personal applications.

2 minutes ┄┄→ Wrap-Up
Review main points.

10 minutes ┄┄→ Celebrations and Concerns
Take time to share.

5 minutes ┄┄→ Closing
Pray together.

1½ hours total ←

Synago: Calm in the Storm

How to Use This Resource

This book is one in a series of resources that will help you successfully begin and continue an effective small group ministry for senior high youth. Each volume gives sixteen sessions (a semester's worth) that are topical Bible studies. Each volume has the same start-up information and helps for student leaders, so you may begin with any volume. Both of the student leaders and the adults who are working with the group(s) will want to have a copy.

Synago: *Light in the Dark*
(student leader)
ISBN: 0687049334
Synago: *Calm in the Storm*
(student leader)
ISBN: 0687049237

For future volumes, see ileadyouth.com.

The **training video** is also for both the adults working with the group(s) and the student leaders. It is best to view it together so that both the leaders and adults understand their roles and responsibilities and can fully support one another.

Synago Training Video
ISBN:0687050235

The **small group notebook** is the hands-on piece for everyone. Provide copies to student leaders, adult counselors, and the other youth members of each small group. The notebook contains the Scripture readings for each session, personal reflection and response activities for the week, and space for note taking and recording prayer requests.

Synago: *Light in the Dark* (student notebook)
ISBN: 0687049733
Synago: *Calm in the Storm* (student notebook)
ISBN: 0687049539

For future volumes, see ileadyouth.com.

The **introductory video** is a great way to generate excitement and support for starting your student-led small group ministry. Use it to recruit student leaders and adult counselors and to publicize your small group ministry to parents, pastors, and others whose support you'll need.

Synago Introductory Video
ISBN: 068704913X

Tips

Check for Fit

Carefully and prayerfully read through this resource to determine if it offers you a model and study material that fits your vision for senior high small group ministry. If it does, use it with the Spirit's guidance to develop your own small group ministry for senior high youth.

Recruit and Train, Practice and Publicize

Use the info in the "Getting Started" and "Help for Student Leaders" sections (pages 9–19 and 22–29) to recruit and train student leaders and adult counselors. You have permission to photocopy certain pages, as noted, in these sections for overhead transparencies and handouts you may want to use for orientation or training. A very effective way to do training is for potential leaders and counselors to experience being a small group. Use one or more of the small group sessions for practice and/or to show what the small group meetings will be like.

Who's Who: Student Leader Roles and Responsibilities

There are two student leaders for each small group; they share the leadership responsibilities, taking turns preparing for and leading the weekly meeting.

Length of Service: One academic year, or through the end of current school year

Qualities: Committed Christian who actively seeks to grow in and live out the Christian faith*; is willing to be discipled as a Christian and trained as a group leader; attends church regularly; relates well with others; is responsible; is a "team player"; is a good communicator; desires to see friends and peers learn about, experience, and grow in the Christian faith; is willing and able to make the time commitment needed for this role.

Responsibilities:
- Attends weekly small group meeting and small group leadership meetings, as scheduled.
- Prepares for the meeting. One leader is responsible for facilitating (session material provided in this resource). The other leader is responsible for the other meeting preparations and follow-up (listed below). These roles alternate each week or the leaders may take turns leading different sections within each session.
- Invites non-Christian friends, Christian friends not active in a church (or who attend a church with few youth opportunities), and youth in need of a loving and caring group of friends; encourages other group members to do this too.
- Reminds group members and potential visitors of meeting time and location.
- Helps arrange transportation for those who need it.
- If facilitating, prepares for the session using the material provided in this resource and the student notebook. (The leader who isn't facilitating still reads through the session material to be prepared to participate in the discussion and help the facilitator if needed.)
- Records attendance and collects visitor contact information; if there is a small group coordinator, forwards the information to him or her within two days.

- Follows up with visitors within two days (by calling, e-mailing, or talking to them at school).
- Follows up with those absent.
- Keeps small group coordinator updated about condition and progress of group.
- Prays regularly for the group and group members.
- Reaches out to group members in special need of the support and care of a Christian friend.
- Encourages group members to have a positive attitude towards the group growing and "multiplying."
- Keeps an eye out for potential new student leaders from within the group.
- Works with co-leader, counselor, and small group coordinator to plan how the group can "multiply" when it reaches ten regular members and works to make the transition a smooth one.

*Note to Student Leaders:
Your desire as a Christian, especially as a small group leader, is to live in such a way that others will see the qualities and "fruit" of a Christian life. Try as hard as you can to not do or say anything that would cause others to question your commitment or that might encourage them to do or say things that are unChristian. We're talking about anything that could harm your (or your peers') relationship with God or with others, or that could harm yourself or others—like drinking, smoking, abusing drugs, lying, fighting, gossiping, being sexually promiscuous, cheating, cursing, and so on. A leader cannot be a "roller coaster" Christian — one who professes a commitment to Christ and acts very devout at times, then parties like crazy on the weekend. Your group members, and peers who may be observing you from a distance, are checking out whether your words match your actions. They want to see if your faith is real. If you're a fake, they will know it, and you'll lose credibility and integrity as a small group leader and as a follower of Christ. However, nobody is perfect, and you will mess up. But don't give up! As Christians, we know that "if we confess our sins, [God] will forgive our sin, because we can trust God to do what is right. God will cleanse us from all the wrongs we have done" (1 John 1:9, NIV). Seek the support of your small group, your counselor, small group coordinator, and youth director to help you grow in Christian maturity and to faithfully live out your commitment.

Who's Who: Adult Roles and Responsibilities

Person in Charge: Vision Keeper

- Shapes and communicates the vision for the small group ministry, its purpose, and how it fits into the total youth ministry program.
- Takes overall responsibility for the small group ministry, in terms of leader accountability, resources, training, spiritual nurture. In other words, "the buck stops here."
- Has a good idea of what is going on in general, but not closely involved in the details of individual groups.
- Guides and helps student leaders, counselors, and coordinators as needed.
- Plans and leads small group leadership meetings.
- Communicates information about small groups to potential group members and provides a way for senior high youth at the church to indicate their interest in being in a group. (Can delegate this task to a small group coordinator.)

> In some situations the vision keeper, coordinator, and counselor roles can all be handled by one person. But plan to grow. Share the vision. Bring other adults on board so that as the numbers of groups grow, adults will be ready to support the ministry.

Small Group Coordinator

Length of Service: One academic year, or through the end of current school year

Qualities: Committed Christian who actively seeks to grow in and live out the Christian faith, attends church regularly, relates well with others, is a good communicator, has administrative and organizational abilities, is interested in discipling students, and is willing to commit the time and energy needed for this role.

Responsibilities:

- Supervises, nurtures, and encourages the leadership of one to four small groups.
- Serves as liaison between his or her small groups and the youth director or whoever is the vision keeper.
- Helps plan and lead orientation and training events.
- Helps with small group leadership meetings.
- Guides and helps student leaders and counselors with issues or problems in their groups or their personal lives.

- Keeps up with the attendance and membership numbers of his or her small groups, tracking to anticipate when it is time to "birth" new groups.
- Helps groups that are "multiplying" by working with leaders and counselors in choosing and training new leadership, deciding who's in the new groups and who their leaders and counselors will be, and doing whatever is needed for a smooth transition.
- Keeps current roster of members of his or her groups, along with address, phone number, e-mail, and other info; forwards this to the youth director for updating youth database.
- Provides leaders with visitor cards or other tool for collecting and reporting visitor info (name, address, phone, e-mail, school, grade, parents, church affiliation, who invited them, and so on).
- Substitutes for counselors at group meetings when needed.
- Regularly contacts his or her student leaders and counselors to keep up with what's happening in their groups.

Adult Counselor

The adult counselor is the key behind-the-scenes person who supports the student leaders by encouraging and advising them and being a caring adult friend.

The counselor doesn't prepare or lead the session. Rather, he or she participates on the same level as the student small group members.

Although the counselor can speak from an adult perspective—and the students may, at times, specifically ask for that perspective—the counselor should not monopolize the discussion, act as a facilitator, or "take the stage" as the one with the "right" answers.

Length of Service:
One academic year, or through the end of current school year

Qualities:
Committed Christian, actively seeks to grow in and live out the Christian faith, attends church regularly, relates well to others, is a good communicator, is interested in discipling students, is willing and able to make the time commitment needed for this role.

Responsibilities:
- Supports and encourages student leaders as an adult Christian friend; affirms their leadership and offers helpful input; checks regularly to see how they're doing and to encourage their spiritual growth; holds them accountable for actively seeking spiritual growth and fulfilling their leader responsibilities.
- Attends weekly group meetings and leadership meetings, as scheduled.

- Finds another adult to substitute for him or her at a small group meeting if he or she has to miss. (The substitute could be the small group coordinator, another counselor, or the youth director.)
- Reviews the session material to prepare for the discussion and to help and encourage the student leaders, as needed.
- Follows up with student leaders to make sure that the session is prepared, home is lined up, and the meeting time and place are communicated to group members.
- Encourages leaders to specifically invite non-Christian friends and Christian friends not active in a church (or who attend a church with few youth opportunities), and youth in need of a loving and caring group of friends.
- Reaches out to group members in special need of the support and care of an adult Christian friend.
- Encourages leaders to have a positive attitude toward the group growing and "multiplying."
- Keeps an eye out for potential new student leaders from within the group.
- Collects visitor information (address, phone, e-mail, school, grade, parent(s), church affiliation, group member who invited them, and so forth).
- Writes or calls the parent(s) of visitors to introduce self and give general information about the small group, sponsoring church, and answer any questions.
- Updates small group coordinator about condition and progress of group, student leaders, and any group members in special need.

Most groups do very well with only one counselor. However, groups also benefit from having a male and a female adult with them. When recruiting, consider inviting a couple to fill this role.

Q Is *Synago* just for large churches?

A Any church, large or small, can launch a small group ministry. Since this design is friendship based, a church is not limited by its youth membership base. The only limitation is the number of Christian youth committed to growing in their faith and willing to take on the leading and nurturing of a group of their friends and by the number of adults willing to serve as counselors. Where two or three are gathered together, there can be a small group.

Q Why don't we just do *Synago* on Sunday morning at the church?

A For many youth, small groups help break barriers to connecting to the church—barriers caused by unfamiliarity, a negative church experience in the past, or negative stereotypes of church or of Christians. Once a youth has reached high school, it's awkward for him or her to suddenly start showing up at youth group or Sunday school. With a small group, youth grow close to the other members. Then going to a larger fellowship of youth—such as Sunday school, youth group, retreats, and worship—isn't so intimidating because they know their friends from the small group are there. Doing announcements in the small group and adding the members to e-mail and mailing lists are ways to continue to invite them to participate in other youth activities and in the congregation.

Q Is *Synago* for all of the high school students in our church?

A Starting a small group ministry doesn't mean stopping Sunday school, youth group, or whatever else your church is offering older youth. This new ministry simply adds a different dimension to what is already in place. *Synago* may not be for all of those who are already active; but some youth will be ready for the greater challenge of leadership, and others will desire the intimacy of a small group. *Synago* may also reach some older youth who have not had their needs met in existing programs and consequently have stopped coming. These youth may find this format to be more what they need. In addition, *Synago* may reach new youth. The in-home, small group setting provides a way for youth—especially those who would never darken the door of a church—to connect and grow spiritually. This friendship-based model offers a unique avenue for evangelism and for greater discipleship.

Q Do we have to do the sessions in order?

A There is a flow to the sessions in each book. The early ones intentionally provide opportunities for the members to get to know one another better. The last one gives the group some closure. However, each session stands on its own. New youth will be coming into the group at different points in the life of the group. So, what is more important than the order of the sessions is the "order" of the group—the atmosphere of caring and of learning together. Do the sessions in the order that makes sense to you as the leaders.

Q Our group has gotten so close. Do we really have to split up?

A The first time your group grows to the point that it needs to "multiply" will be challenging. But if a group grows too large, many of the benefits of being small and close-knit are lost. One reason for repeating the Purpose Statement at each meeting is to prepare the group. The leaders' having a positive attitude and also involving the group in deciding how to divide are crucial to making the multiplying go smoothly. When your group is ready to multiply, have a "birth day" celebration.

Help for Student Leaders

A Word of Encouragement: You Can Do It!

Feeling a little nervous about leading a small group? A bit overwhelmed? Wondering if you'll be able to keep discussions alive? What if friends you invite don't come? What if you get asked questions about God or Jesus or the Bible and you don't know the answers? Don't worry. You can do this! Here's why:

- **You've been chosen.** Someone has seen in you a love for God, devotion to Jesus Christ, a desire to grow spiritually, and compassion for your teenage peers. Someone already believes in your ability to be a small group leader. That's why you were asked to be a student leader. Jesus Christ has also chosen you, as one of his disciples. He will equip you and empower you as you seek to live as his follower and to use your gifts and abilities in his service.

- **You are not alone.** You will have the support and encouragement of others—your co-leader, counselor, small group coordinator, and youth director or pastor. Call on them when you need advice, help, or just a friend to talk to. You are part of a ministry team.

- **You don't have to be an expert.** A student leader should have a love for God's Word, not a mastery of it. You should have a desire to learn more about the Bible and how to apply its truth and teachings to your life. You'll learn a lot about the Bible as you prepare to lead your group, and you'll have opportunities to share information that may be helpful to others during your study of biblical passages. If you're asked a question you can't answer, just promise to check into it and get back with what you find out. Perhaps someone else in the group has an answer. If not, do a little research (Bible commentaries, pastor or other Christian adult) and report what you find out.

- **You can learn.** Your training as a student leader and the tips provided in this resource will help prepare you to lead meaningful and productive discussions. You'll also get practical advice at leadership meetings, as you and other small group leaders talk about what works in your groups and exchange ideas. You'll also become better at facilitating as you gain experience and get to know and understand your group's dynamics.

- **You can expect great meetings and not-so-great meetings.** Sometimes even the best preparation and most skillful discussion-leading won't result in a great meeting. Sometimes your group may just be in a funk and not be talkative—or the opposite—everyone has the sillies and can't get serious. You may have a meeting where, for whatever reasons, you have a much lower turn-out than normal. Sometimes there may be distractions over which you have no control. "Dud" meetings aren't a sign of personal failure on your part. They just happen. Keep a positive attitude, and don't be discouraged. Consider what God can teach you through the experience.

- **You have something special to offer—yourself.** No one is in a better position to reach out to and connect with your friends and peers than YOU. They know you; they like you; they trust you. You'll be an awesome student leader, if you're willing to just be yourself—a Christian teen who doesn't have all the answers, but who does have a faith story to share; who isn't perfect, but who believes in forgiveness and hanging in there; and who is kind and compassionate to others.

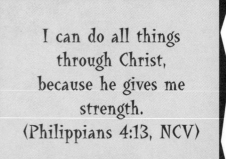

I can do all things through Christ, because he gives me strength.
(Philippians 4:13, NCV)

Getting Ready to Lead

Session Prep

Start preparing days (not hours) before your small group meeting. Putting time into your preparation

1. reflects your commitment to the group;
2. helps you to be mentally and spiritually ready to lead and participate in the session;
3. makes it less likely that you will forget something (like supplies, or letting group members know of a location change); and
4. results in a more smoothly-run session, as you have time to get comfortable with the session material and are better able to encourage and contribute to the discussion.

By getting an early start on your preparation, you'll also have time to consult with your counselor, in case you have any questions or concerns. Although you can do a lot of the prep work by yourself, you and your co-leader should spend some time preparing together and sharing the responsibilities, so you know who's doing what and can make sure that nothing on the checklist gets overlooked.

Personal Prep

Try to spend at least ten to fifteen minutes a day with God in a personal devotional time. Your *Synago* Notebook has some questions and activities for reflection and response that you can use for devotionals. The group members will be doing them the week after your meeting, but you will find that doing them the week before is helpful to you as you lead.

You may also use a devotional book or read a Bible passage that you can pray about, reflect on, and/or write about in a journal. Spend time each day praying to God, expressing thanks and praise, confessing your sins, and asking for forgiveness and guidance. Pray for your own needs and for those of your small group members. Pray for your session time together.

Last Minute Details!

- Get your supplies—pens, *Synago* Notebooks, extra Bibles, and so on.
- Arrive fifteen minutes early. You need to have time to greet the host family, set up the meeting area, get focused, and welcome group members as they arrive.
- Set up the meeting area so everyone can sit in a circle. Control for distractions, such as TV and stereo, pets or children, and phones.

R&R in the Synago Notebook

Every participant should have a notebook. It contains the Scripture, a place for notes, room to write in prayer requests—and some simple R&R (Reflect and Respond) for during the week. As part of your closing time each session, remind the participants of the R&R section and invite them to continue their spiritual growth between meetings.

If for some reason your planned material is not taking as much time as is available, turn to the R&R directions in the notebook for more ideas for the session. Doing R&R together is a good way to encourage one another to develop some practices that will continue to help you grow in your faith and devotion to God.

Weekly Checklist

These things need to happen before each meeting. Coordinate with your co-leader.

___ Maintain **attendance** record of last meeting.

___ Give a **thank-you call** to the host parents of your last meeting location.

___ Follow up, within two days, with **visitors** to your last meeting (by phone, e-mail, card, talking at school). This means telling them you're glad they came and appreciated their participation; giving them additional info about the group or answering any questions they may have; inviting them to come again; asking if they have anything going on in their lives that you can be praying about for them.

___ Find out if anyone needs a ride; help make **arrangements**, if necessary.

___ If you have a new, regular group member, get a **Synago Notebook** for him or her.

___ Bring some **Bibles**. The Scriptures are all printed in the *Synago* Notebook, so everyone can read them easily with no one being embarrassed about not knowing where to find them in the Bible. But as participants grow more confident, encourage them to bring and use their Bibles or the ones on hand. Besides, it's fun and often very helpful to see how the different versions translate a passage.

___ Follow up with group **members who missed** the last meeting.

___ Confirm the **next meeting place** (home) and refreshments.

___ Contact (call, e-mail, tell at school) **group members** to make sure that they know where you're meeting. Remind them to bring their *Synago* Notebooks (or Bibles).

___ As often as you can, invite **friends and acquaintances** who are non-Christians, not involved with a church, or Christian youth having personal struggles. You set an important example for others in your group. If you don't invite anyone, why should they? Encourage your group members to be invitational by your words and your actions.

___ Check in with your **counselor**. Evaluate your last meeting. Go over anything you need to for the next one.

___ Think about and get any **supplies** you may need.

___ Work through the **session material** for the next meeting. Highlight key points; do some research on unfamiliar words, phrases, verses. The *Synago* Notebook includes the text for the Bible passages and has margin notes with helpful information. You can also look the texts up in a Bible dictionary or commentary. Talk to your counselor, small group coordinator, or youth director, or pastor about anything you don't understand or want more information on. It's great to ask questions! That's how you learn!

Synago: Calm in the Storm

Bible Study Tools You Can Use

The Bible

Although the Scripture for each session is printed in the *Synago* Notebook, you need a Bible to help prepare for the "Word Search" (Bible study) part of your small group meeting. You also need a Bible for your personal reading, study, and devotional times. Some Bibles are easier to read and understand than others. In fact, some Bibles are designed especially for youth. Here are some things to keep in mind when getting a Bible:

Translation—In a Bible translation, the original Hebrew or Greek text has been translated into another language, like English. Some translations you may have heard of are the New Revised Standard Version (NRSV), New International Version (NIV), New King James Version (NJKV), and the Contemporary English Version (CEV). But how can you have several translations of the same text, you ask? Say you've been given a story in your Spanish class that you have to translate from Spanish into English. When all the papers are turned in, the translations may differ slightly according to the words and phrases different students choose to use. Sometimes reading the same passage in different versions can help make the meaning clearer.

Paraphrase—A paraphrase of the Bible tends to be written in contemporary language, making it readable, colorful, and easy to understand. Unlike a translation, it isn't a direct translation of the original. Instead, a paraphrase restates what the text means. Paraphrases use contemporary words, phrases, metaphors, and images that have meaning within the times and culture of the reader, not the times and culture of the writings. *The Message* and *The Living Bible* are examples of paraphrases.

Study Bible—A study Bible is available in different translations. It has notes on specific Bible verses, definitions of unfamiliar words, and information on Bible people, Bible lands, and Bible times to help you understand the meaning and interpretation of biblical texts. Some study Bibles also have devotional material and questions for reflection and personal application.

Dictionaries and Commentaries

These books are like having a knowledgeable person right there to help you answer questions or give another viewpoint.

Bible Dictionary—This gives definitions for tons of words found in the Bible. This is especially helpful if you don't have a study Bible.

Commentary—This resource gives you someone's scholarly understanding and interpretation of Scripture. It includes explanations and cultural information, as well as information about who probably wrote the text, why, and for whom it was written. Commentaries can help you understand why certain stories were told, events recorded, or teachings given and what significance they had for the original audience (who heard them about two thousand years ago in the Middle East). If you don't have a Bible commentary at home, try your church or a library.

Voice, Audience, Context

In your role as a student leader, you're expected to spend time learning what you can about the Scripture passage for the session, so you can help others in your group gain a better understanding or help them consider a different meaning or interpretation. Your preparation should include determining the voice, audience, and context of the text your group is studying.

Voice—Who was the writer? Or who is "speaking" in the passage?

Audience—Who was listening? Who were the ones hearing the words originally? For whom was the text originally written?

Context—What comes before and after the text? How does this add to the meaning and significance of the text? Also what was the society of that time like? What was the context in which the people lived and would have understood what was being said? What do you know about the times and the people back then?

Answering these questions also helps prevent prooftexting. Prooftexting is taking Scripture out of context and applying it or using it in a way that wasn't originally intended or that is inconsistent with the overall message of the Bible—the story of God's love for us.

Discussion Tips

One reason your group members will keep coming to your small group is the opportunity to talk with friends about a topic of personal interest and share things of a personal nature in a safe and confidential environment. You, as a student leader, are key to creating that environment by reminding everyone of the confidential nature of the discussions and by encouraging honesty and openmindedness. Here are some specific suggestions to get them talking and to keep them coming back to your small group meetings!

DO know that your role is to facilitate, or help, not to be an expert. In other words, you don't have to have all the answers! Your job is to encourage sharing and reflection among group members, presenting helpful information that will add to their understanding and ability to participate. Although you have prepared for the session and done some research on the biblical text, it's very likely that someone will ask a question to which you don't know the answer. When that happens, toss it back to the group and see if anyone else has a response. You can also offer to look into it, or have another member check it out, and come back the next week with some more information. This gives you time to check with your youth director, pastor, or another source who may be able to help you. You may also be dealing with a question that you just need to say is "unanswerable."

DON'T be afraid of silence. To give thoughtful, honest answers, group members will often need time to reflect and think of what they want to say. If you feel the silence is getting too long, try rephrasing the question. If the answer involves some personal sharing, you may need to go first (which is why you need to have thought through your own answers ahead of time!). Your example of being open, honest, vulnerable, and trusting will encourage others to be the same.

DO try to avoid the student/teacher syndrome. Since you've already prepared your own responses to the questions, you may be tempted to want to give your answers first, especially if you encounter some silence. Resist that temptation. Instead, be OK with a little silence, encourage your friends to take some time to reflect, or ask "What do you guys think?" Sometimes, group members may try to give you the answer they think you're looking for—an answer that "sounds" right. For example, if you're asking a question about the biblical text, they may look at you as they answer to see if they got it "right." Although there will be some key points that certain questions will attempt to bring out in the discussion, try to work in these points yourself only if others haven't.

DON'T be judgmental or critical about others' comments. (In other words, don't laugh at a comment that wasn't meant to be funny; don't express horror, shock, or disgust with what someone says; don't say, "That is so stupid; where did you get that idea?" or "I can't believe you really believe that!") Set an example of openmindedness and encourage it in the discussion. If someone says something insensitive, insulting, or really surprising, ask if anyone else has a response (without being insensitive or insulting themselves). Sometimes you may need to help group members decide to "agree to disagree" about something. You may also want to ask follow-up questions to help individuals consider why they have a particular belief or opinion and where it came from.

DO "peel the onion." Sometimes people have difficulty expressing themselves or communicating what they mean. If you don't understand a group member's comment, you may need to ask follow-up questions to help him or her explain an answer. You can "peel the onion," or get more info from someone, by asking questions like, "Can you give me an example of what you're talking about?"; "I think I know what you're getting at, but I'm not sure. Can you think of another way to say that to help me understand?" "That's a very interesting way of looking at it. What helped you come up with that interpretation?"

DO control gossips, side conversations, and discussion hogs. These are major discussion killers. This may be hard for you to do as a student leader, because the people in your group are your peers. It's uncomfortable for many teens to act like an authority figure with their friends. But as a group leader, it is your responsibility, not the adult counselor's, to keep the discussion focused, moving along, and productive. It is also your job to promote a safe and confidential environment, so that group members will want to talk. You, your co-leader, and counselor should come up with strategies for dealing with these situations, with specific ideas for what to say or do. You may even want to address this in your group and get group members' input on how do deal with these situations when they happen. If you have an ongoing problem with one or more individuals and none of your strategies have worked, then speak with them privately and in a nonjudgmental manner, relating your concerns and suggesting how they can help.

DO know when to ask and when to wait. Sometimes it's OK to ask specific group members to respond and sometimes you need to let a question "hang out there" for voluntary answers. There are questions in each session that everyone should feel comfortable answering. These questions have an asterisk (*) by them. Encourage each person to answer these. ("OK, guys, this is a question for each of us to answer"; "Joe, we haven't heard from you. How would you answer this question?") But, of course, you can't force someone to answer, and you never want to make anyone feel uncomfortable for choosing not to participate.

Most of the session questions, however, are designed for group members to answer voluntarily. (Introduce those questions with, "This next one's for the whole group." Or follow-up the question with, "Does anyone else have an answer for this one?")

Also, make sure that you only ask volunteers to read the biblical text in the session. Some people just aren't comfortable reading out loud, and you might not know who is or who isn't. Same goes for prayer. You may want to ask for volunteers to open and close your closing prayer time. During this time, prayer is offered aloud voluntarily. There are some options for the closing prayer, however, that do require each person to participate. Typically, though, this only involves saying a one-word prayer or praying for someone by just repeating a phrase or mentioning a name (like, "Pray for the person on your right by saying, 'Thank you, God, for _____.' ").

DO encourage and set an example of being a good listener. Don't have a side conversation with your co-leader while someone in your group is talking. Show compassion and understanding; be honest and open. Also be openminded and accepting of opinions and beliefs that differ from or are even in conflict with yours.

DO watch the clock; keep the discussion focused. This will be hard. Group discussions can easily jump from one topic to another, taking up lots of time and getting way off track. Plus, some people are just long-winded. Keep the discussion moving and focused. As you prepare for the session, have a good idea of how much time to spend on each part. (You may even want to write down the times in the margin, such as "7:15–7:20" beside "Warm-Up.") Decide, in advance, which questions you may need to "ax," if you run short on time. The goal is to make sure you don't spend so much time on the Warm-Up and Topic Talk sections (which group members can really get into), that you run out of time for the biblical study, reflection, sharing of personal concerns, and prayer time. These are the sections that provide the most opportunities for your group to talk about things that are private, to share their faith stories and experiences, to be reflective, and to show love and concern to each other as a faith community.

DO consistently stress the importance of confidentiality. If anyone tells something said in small group to a friend, parent, teacher, coach who isn't in the group, then confidentiality is violated. This can kill a small group. If this happens, depending on the nature of what was told, you and your co-leader and counselor must decide how to respond. The only exception to the rule of confidentiality is when a group member says something that indicates that he or she or others may be in danger. (This includes references to suicide, abuse, harming self or others, or running away.) If this happens, the counselor should give this information to the youth director or pastor, who will determine the appropriate action.

Ways to Close in Prayer

Choose in Advance

Most of the sessions give you the choice of how to close in prayer. In making that choice, you'll need to consider the number of persons in your group (a lot or a few, since this affects your time), make up of group (comfort level with praying aloud), session topic, and amount of remaining time. Because you can't predict what can happen in a session that will affect the timing and mood, you'll need to be flexible and ready to adapt or change your prayer closing.

Write 'Em Down

Before your closing prayer, your group will spend time sharing personal celebrations (great things that have recently happened, answered prayer) and prayer concerns (things for which they'd like the group to pray). During this time, you and the other members should write down the specific prayer requests in your *Synago* Notebooks so you can pray for these concerns during the week.

Encourage Others

Your closing prayer time is a great opportunity to encourage your group in their own prayer life. Some members may feel they aren't "good" at praying. (Maybe you feel that way!) This is a good time to remind everyone that prayer is simply talking to God. You don't need to use certain words or sound eloquent. God already knows our requests before we ask. It's not the words that make great prayers; it's the honesty and sincerity with which they're offered. Encourage the group just to pray as if they were talking to a close friend.

Options For Closing Prayers

Solo Prayer
A leader or member prays. This style is best to use when you're running short on time—but don't overuse it!

Pulse Prayer
Everyone holds hands. Starting with a leader and moving to the person on the right, each person prays either aloud *or* silently. When finished, each person squeezes the hand of the person to his or her right, indicating it's that person's turn to pray. The last person closes with "Amen."

Shared Prayer
After group members have given prayer concerns, the leader asks for a volunteer to choose and pray for a specific concern. (For example, Zach volunteers to pray for Meredith's sick grandmother.) The last person to pray should cover any concern not already prayed for by other group members.

Popcorn Prayer
Ask for two volunteers to open and close the prayer. (If you know some people in your group who are comfortable praying aloud, you may want to ask them. Just don't have the same people opening and closing all the time.) After someone has opened in prayer, anyone who wants to pray aloud does so at will. Persons can "go" more than once. When a long silence indicates the group's readiness to close, the "closer" wraps up.

Prayer Box
Have a small box or basket or cap out during the meeting, along with some pens and scratch paper. Encourage persons to write down a prayer request or celebration as one comes to mind and to put it in the prayer box. They can include their name with their request or remain anonymous. You could also choose to have members do this during the "Celebrations and Concerns" time. For the closing prayer, each person picks one of the prayer requests and prays aloud for it. Remind the group that praying for the request can be simply reading it aloud from the paper, perhaps with a follow-up chorus of "Hear our prayer, O Lord."

Reading the Purpose Statement at the beginning of each session is extremely important. If group members have heard it enough to know it by heart, that's even better! Here's why you should not skip opening with reading the Purpose Statement:

- It focuses everyone on why they are a small group and what is supposed to happen in the session. It communicates expectations for personal behavior (honest, openminded, encouraging), goals for personal spiritual growth, and goals for the group to grow together as a body of Christ.

- It keeps the group Christ-centered. Although the meeting provides a place to openly discuss differing opinions, interpretations, and beliefs, the story of the Christian faith and the teachings of Christ take center stage. The discussion is an opportunity to reflect on the Christian faith as it relates to their personal opinions, experiences, and issues.

- It spells out expectations that the group live as a faith community, following biblical teachings for believers. You can call these the "One Another Principles": love one another, be kind to one another, pray for one another, forgive one another, encourage one another.

- It informs visitors that you are a Christian group. Even though your membership is open to and encourages participation of youth who are not Christian or who are not active in church, you want visitors to know up front that they will be exploring life issues in relation to the Christian faith. Your small group members may invite friends by saying that you get together and talk about stuff, leaving out the Jesus Christ part. But by hearing the Purpose Statement, visitors are clearly informed.

- It reaffirms the confidential nature of the group. Group members are reminded of their personal responsibility to keep confidentiality. Stressing this communicates that the small group is a safe place for sharing.

- It communicates the goal to grow in numbers, in order to "multiply" into new groups. Because your members may become very close, they may lose sight of the goal to bring others into the group and may become resistant to growth and change. This mindset leads to a group that is exclusive, rather than invitational. They become more focused on staying together, rather than on sharing with others what they've found in their small group experience. The group is designed to grow. Reading the Purpose Statement reminds your group of this goal, so that when time comes to multiply into two new groups, it's not a shock.

Purpose Statement

The Purposes of Our Small Group Are to

- grow closer in our relationships with God and Jesus Christ;

- grow closer in our relationships with one another;

- learn more about the Christian faith and God's Word;

- encourage honesty and sharing in an atmosphere of trust, confidentiality, and open-mindedness;

- support one another and care for one another in Christian love;

- grow in number by inviting others;

- "multiply" into two groups when we reach 10 regular members to encourage intimacy and continued growth.

Small Group Sessions

Purpose Statement

The purposes of our small group are to

Grow closer in our relationships with God and Jesus Christ;

Grow closer in our relationships with one another;

Learn more about the Christian faith and God's Word;

Encourage honesty and sharing in an atmosphere of trust, confidentiality, and open-mindedness;

Support one another and care for one another in Christian love;

Grow in number by inviting others;

"Multiply" into two groups when we reach 10 regular members to encourage intimacy and continued growth.

Life Issue

Time management

Faith Connection

Putting Christ first in their lives helps Christians set priorities.

Main Ideas

Actually, setting priorities isn't the problem. We usually have a good idea of what should be important in our lives, along with the desire and intent to give those important things the time and attention they deserve. The problem is following through. A day has only so many hours, a week has only so many days. And certain things that we just have to do always seem to fill up our time. When someone suggests, "Well, just cut something out," you may ask, "Like what, the four hours of sleep I'm getting?"

If you aren't one who is feeling pulled apart by commitments and responsibilities, count your blessings. However, if you're like a lot of people nowadays who describe their lives as "busy," take heart. God's Word and the guidance of the Holy Spirit can help you find peace of mind, purpose, and fulfillment.

Begin with an honest, prayerful look at how you spend your time—all of your commitments and responsibilities. Consider your motivations for each. Weigh the costs against the benefits of each. What do you absolutely, positively have to do or participate in now? What can be postponed because the opportunity will be there later? What is important to you that you think you're neglecting? Do you feel a strong urge—perhaps a nudge from God—to give your time and yourself to something else?

God knows the sheer number and variety of choices available to you that compete for your time, energy, abilities, and resources. Decisions to focus on schoolwork, sports and other school activities, a job, volunteering, helping at home, being with friends, and so forth are not bad choices. But when they squeeze out time for God and for Christian fellowship, service, and worship, then your spiritual life suffers and the faith community is affected by your absence. When you seek God's help in setting priorities and you are willing to act on that guidance by making some tough choices (maybe choices that disappoint or don't make sense to friends or family), then life will be just as full but more meaningful, purposeful, and rewarding.

Read, Research, Reflect
Luke 10:38-42; Matthew 6:33

Read the Scripture and additional info in your *Synago* Notebook. Make notes on the following:

- Who is "speaking" or telling the story in each passage? Who is the intended audience? What is the context? (What do you think the situation is? What's happening before and after each passage?)
- Pray about and reflect on the readings. What do they say to you?

Memorize

"But strive first for the kingdom of God and his righteousness, and all these things will be given to you as well."
(Matthew 6:33, NRSV)

Prepare

- Note your own answers to the questions.
- Decide how you'll close in prayer. (See "Ways to Close in Prayer," page 28.)
- Get supplies.

Supplies:
Synago Notebook for each person, pencils or pens, paper, Bibles or copies of the Bible readings and note cards for those who don't have a *Synago* Notebook

* Questions with an * should be answered by everyone.

Opening   **5 minutes**

Welcome/Announcements/Purpose Statement/Prayer

Warm-Up   **10 minutes**

Invite group members to answer two to three of the following questions. Stay within the time limit! *

• Would you rather own a dog or a cat?*
• Would you rather have the power to fly or the power to become invisible?*
• Would you rather do something you hate and make $100,000 a year or something you love and make $20,000 a year?*

Topic Talk   **15 minutes**

Hand out paper and pencils or pens. Allow three minutes for group members to either list activities or draw a pie chart showing how they spend their time in a typical week. Have them focus on those activities that take up significant amounts of time. Write estimates as to how much time is given to these activities during a week.

1. Report your "actual" priorities to the group, based on your estimates of how you spend your time.*

2. What factors have had the greatest influence on how you spend your time? (Examples: what parents or friends want you to do, personal goals, personal interests, personal values, financial needs, academic needs)*

Word Search   **Luke 10:38-42; Matthew 6:33**   **15 minutes**

Ask a volunteer to read Luke 10:38-42 aloud. Tell group members the background information you have about the setting of the story and about Mary and Martha. Refer to the note at the bottom of page 8 in the Notebook.

1. According to the reading, what was Mary doing while Jesus was visiting? What was Martha doing? Why do you think they responded to his visit in such different ways?

2. What did Martha ask Jesus? Why?

3. How did Jesus answer Martha (verses 41-42)? What do you think about his response?

4. What do you think Jesus means by "the better part" (verse 42)?

Have another volunteer read Matthew 6:33 aloud.

5. a. What do you think "the kingdom of God" refers to?
   b. What do you think God's "righteousness" is?
   c. What are some things that will be "given to you as well"?

R and R—Reflect and Respond 20 minutes

1. If Jesus came to visit you, what tasks would "distract" you or keep you from spending time with him? (Would he even find you at home?)*

2. What presents the biggest obstacles to seeking God's help in setting priorities? (Examples: cutting back on doing something you enjoy; taking a risk to do what God wants, being unsure of what God wants; disappointing others; difficulty in saying no when asked to do something; trusting God rather than self to provide for needs)

3. What specific problem or struggle are you having with priorities right now? What changes may God be calling you to make? Why?*

4. What are some guidelines in setting priorities that reflect faith and trust in God and a desire to do God's will?

Wrap-Up 2 minutes

God knows the sheer number and variety of choices available to you that compete for your time, energy, abilities, and resources. Decisions to focus on schoolwork, sports and other school activities, a job, volunteering, helping at home, being with friends, and so forth are not bad choices. But when they squeeze out time for God and for Christian fellowship, service, and worship, then your spiritual life suffers and the faith community is affected by your absence—your presence and unique gifts and abilities are missed. When you seek God's help in setting priorities and you are willing to act on that guidance by making some tough choices (maybe choices that disappoint or don't make sense to friends or family), then life will be just as full but more meaningful, purposeful, and rewarding.

Read aloud or restate in your own words.

Celebrations and Concerns 5 minutes

Invite group members to share celebrations and concerns.

Closing Prayer 10 minutes

Pray especially for group members' decisions about priorities.

Setting Priorities

Life Issue

Appreciating nature; caring for the earth

Faith Connection

In the beauty, majesty, and intricacies of the earth and its life forms, Christians marvel at the God who created it all. We serve as caretakers to protect and maintain the world God created for us to live in, live on, live with, and enjoy.

Main Ideas

Some of the most meaningful faith experiences Christians have are when they contemplate the greatness of God through their encounters with the natural world. What is more awe-inspiring than a brilliant sunset, the rhythmic crashing of ocean waves, the vast expanse of the plains, the birth of a kitten, the design of a spider's web, the spirit-lifting height of a mountain peak?

Our God is a Creator-God, and we often feel a connection to God as our Creator when we "get back" to nature. As we reflect on our experiences with the natural world, we can appreciate God as creative, detail-conscious, greater than we can understand, and intentional. (Just think about how the human body works!)

When we stop focusing on ourselves and ponder, instead, the complexity of a microscopic cell or the seeming endlessness of the night sky or the busy intensity of a honeybee, we take notice of the God of the universe and the world God created for our use and pleasure. As God's children, we respond faithfully by giving God our praise and our thanks and by caring for our world and the creatures with which we share it.

Read, Research, Reflect

Psalm 104:1-13, 19-23, 31-33

Read the Scripture and additional info in your *Synago* Notebook. Make notes on the following:

- Who is "speaking" or telling the story in each passage? Who is the intended audience? What is the context? (What do you think the situation is? What's happening before and after each passage?)
- Pray about and reflect on the readings. What do they say to you?

Memorize

"You look at the earth, and it trembles. You touch the mountains, and smoke goes up. As long as I live, I will sing and praise you, the LORD God."

(Psalm 104:32-33 CEV)

Prepare

- Note your own answers to the questions.
- Decide how you'll close in prayer. (See page 28.)
- Get supplies (don't forget the nature items).

Back to Nature

Supplies: Items from nature for group members to hold (such as flowers, leaves, sea shells, small rocks, snake skin, bird's nest), *Synago* Notebook for each person; pencils or pens, Bibles or copies of the Bible readings and note cards for those who don't have a Synago Notebook.

* Questions with an * should be answered by everyone.

Opening 5 minutes

Welcome/Announcements/Purpose Statement/Prayer

Warm-Up 5 minutes

If given the choice, would you rather spend time in the mountains or at the coast? Why?*

Topic Talk 15 minutes

Hand out the nature items so that each group member has one to hold in his or her hand or lap during the session. They're just reminders of the variety of things God has created in the world.

1. What is something in nature that really amazes you? (Examples: a microscopic organism, a sunset, the ocean, birth, the stars, a tornado, ants carrying things ten times their weight)*

2. In what ways do you connect God with nature?

3. Tell about a time when you experienced God's presence through an encounter with nature. (Examples: on a rock climbing trip, while looking at the stars in your backyard, while watching a puppy being born, while walking on the beach during a retreat, while watching a sunset from an airplane window)

4. Name one positive thing you think humans are doing to care for the world and one thing that concerns you.*

Word Search 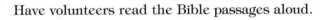Psalm 104:1-13, 19-23, 31-33 15 minutes

Have volunteers read the Bible passages aloud.

1. How would you describe the tone of this writing? In what mood was the author?

2. What do you think was the author's purpose in writing this psalm?

3. If you didn't know anything about God, how would this reading affect your understanding of what God is like?

Back to Nature

R and R—Reflect and Respond   **15 minutes**

1. a. In what ways can thinking about or experiencing nature enrich or influence a Christian's faith?*
   b. How does nature influence or enrich your own faith?*

2. Should Christians be active in protecting and caring for the world? Why?

3. Which of the following do you think God may be calling you to do to live out your faith?*
   a. intentionally spend more time in nature as a way to experience and reflect on God's presence
   b. be careful not to litter
   c. make environmentally-friendly lifestyle changes in what you buy and use (Be specific.)
   d. become an activist—work to educate others, create awareness, or effect change regarding an environmental issue that's important to you (Like what?)
   e. other (Name it.)

Read aloud or restate in your own words.

Wrap-Up   **2 minutes**

When we take the time to focus less on ourselves and ponder, instead, the complexity of a microscopic cell or the seeming endlessness of the night sky or the busy intensity of a honeybee, we take notice of the God of the universe and the world God created for our use and pleasure. As God's children, we respond in faith by giving God our praise and our thanks and by passionately caring for our world and the creatures with which we share it.

Celebrations and Concerns   **10 minutes**

Invite group members to share celebrations and concerns for others to pray for during the week.

Closing Prayer   **10 minutes**

Use the ACTS of prayer format, but pray specifically for our natural world. Take turns around the circle, as group members say a sentence or phrase prayer for each of the following rounds:

A   Adoration—Praise God as creator (like in Psalm 104:1, "I praise you LORD God, with all my heart. You are glorious and majestic.")
C   Confession—Confess how we neglect or abuse the earth; how we fail to appreciate nature and responsibly care for it.
T   Thanksgiving—Thank God for things God has created or for how God cares for the earth and all living things.
S   Special Requests (or "supplication")—Ask for God's help to personally care for the environment, or pray for a particular environmental concern.

Life Issue

Understanding the Christian concept of forgiveness

Faith Connection

Forgiveness is a basic concept of the Christian faith. God forgives our sin through the sacrificial death of Jesus Christ, thus restoring our relationship with God—a relationship that we damage when we sin. When we forgive people who sin against us, then we are faithfully following the example and teachings of Jesus.

Main Ideas

People can really do you wrong—lie to you, steal from you, gossip about you, get you into trouble, break promises, take advantage of you, hurt you, and turn away from you. They can make you angry and make you cry. Your gut may tell you to get even, but God tells you to forgive. Forgiving people who have sinned against you is one of the hardest things you are called to do as a Christian. But you have to.

Why? The first reason: God forgives us for all the lousy, mean, selfish, offensive, and hurtful things we say and do to God, to others, and even to ourselves. Even though we don't deserve to be forgiven, God forgives us. God wants a relationship with us, but our sin spoils it. When you've done something wrong to someone, the relationship—with God, a family member, a friend, or even a stranger—is damaged. When you say you're sorry, you are saying that you want to do your part to make things right again.

The second reason: Since forgiving people who have wronged you can be such a difficult, going-against-the-culture thing to do, it is a major witness to others of what it means to be a Christian. Some people may never understand the incredible nature of God's forgiveness, unless they experience forgiveness firsthand from you. We show that we are followers of Jesus Christ when we forgive those who sin against us.

What if people who wrong you aren't sorry? Try to forgive them anyway. Forgiving helps us to heal, even if the relationship can't be healed. God doesn't say to forgive and act as if the sin never happened. Although forgiveness is a first step in reconciliation, sometimes you have to end a relationship if it's with someone who continually, and unrepentantly continues to wrong you. Reconciliation can happen only when those who sin against you say that they are sorry, really mean it, and try to change. Let God help you determine when to forgive and reconcile or to forgive and move on without that relationship.

Read, Research, Reflect   1 John 1:8-9; Luke 11:2-4; 17:3b-4; Ephesians 4:32

Read the Scripture and additional info in your *Synago* Notebook. Make notes on who is "speaking" or telling the story in each passage, who the intended audience is, and what the situation is. Pray about and reflect on the readings. What do they say to you?

Memorize

"If we confess our sins, [God] is faithful and just and will forgive us our sins and purify us from all unrighteousness."
(1 John 1:9, NIV)

Prepare

- Note your own answers to the questions.
- Decide what type of prayer you will use for the closing. (See page 28.)
- Get supplies.

Forgiveness   **39**

Supplies: *Synago* Notebook for each person who doesn't have one (or Bibles or copies of the Bible readings and note cards), pencils or pens.

* Questions with an * should be answered by everyone.

Opening   5 minutes

Welcome/Announcements/Purpose Statement/Prayer

Warm-Up   5 minutes

What would be harder to forgive a friend for: lying to you or stealing from you? Why?*

Topic Talk   15 minutes

1. Do you forgive easily or do you tend to hold a grudge?*

2. Without mentioning names, tell about a time when someone really wronged you—a friend, family member, some other person. Did you forgive this person? Why, or why not?* (Leader: Remind the group about the need for confidentiality.)

3. In your experience, when someone wrongs someone else, what are some of the results or consequences?

Word Search   20 minutes

1 John 1:8-9; Luke 11:2-4; 17:3b-4; Ephesians 4:32

Ask a volunteer to read 1 John 1:8-9 aloud.

1. According to this reading, everyone sins—no one is perfect. What can this reading tell us about the nature of God? (Examples: that God is faithful, just, forgiving, purifying)

2. According to verse 9, is there anything you could do that God would not forgive if you confessed that sin?

Ask a volunteer to read Luke 11:2-4 aloud.

3. For what reasons, or for what purpose, do you think Jesus told his followers to seek God's forgiveness daily?

4. In addition to asking for personal forgiveness, what other expectation did Jesus have of his followers? (forgiving others)

Ask a volunteer to read Ephesians 4:32 and Luke 17:3b-4 aloud.

5. Why is the practice of forgiving others such an important aspect and expectation of the Christian life?

6. How are Christians to forgive others?

R&R—Reflect and Respond **25 minutes**

1. Take a moment to consider what life would be like if there were no such thing as forgiveness. Tell your thoughts.

2. Tell about a personal experience of forgiveness that had an impact on your life. (This could be an experience of receiving forgiveness or forgiving someone else.)

3. Tell the group a situation in your life where you are struggling either to confess something and ask for forgiveness or you are struggling to forgive someone who has wronged you.* (Leader: Encourage group members to offer words of encouragement and support.)

Wrap-Up **2 minutes**

Forgiving people who have sinned against us is one of the hardest things we are called to do as Christians. But we have to. First, because God forgives us for all the lousy, mean, selfish, offensive, and hurtful things we say and do to God, to others, and even to ourselves. Even though we don't deserve to be forgiven, God forgives us anyway because God wants a relationship with us—and our sin spoils it. When you tell God you are sorry, you are saying that you want to do your part to make things right again—to put that relationship back on track, to make it better. In the same way, saying that we're sorry to people we have sinned against says we want to mend those relationships, too.

Another reason to forgive others is that it is a major way to witness to your faith. Because forgiving people who have wronged you can be such a difficult, counter-cultural thing to do, it is a powerful witness of your faith to others. Others may never understand the incredible nature of God's forgiveness, unless they experience forgiveness firsthand from you. We show that we are followers of Jesus Christ when we forgive those who sin against us.

Read aloud, or restate in your own words, to the group.

What if people who wrong you aren't sorry? Try to forgive them, anyway. Forgiving helps us heal, even if the relationship cannot be healed. Although forgiveness is a first step in reconciliation, sometimes you have to end a relationship if it is with someone who continues to wrong you and is not really sorry for it. Reconciliation can happen only when those who sin against you are truly sorry and try to change.

Celebrations and Concerns **5 minutes**

If there is time, ask group members to briefly share celebrations and concerns. Otherwise, go directly to the Closing Prayer.

Closing Prayer **5 minutes**

Invite group members to pray silently for a few minutes, confessing their sins to God. Close by thanking God for the hope we have in God's great desire to love us, to forgive us, and to be in an intimate relationship with us. Then read aloud 1 John 1:9 to end the prayer:

"If we confess our sins, [God] is faithful and just and will forgive us our sins and purify us from all unrighteousness." Thank you, God, for your love and forgiveness. Amen"

Forgiveness

When Boy Meets Girl

Life Issue

Gender differences

Faith Connection

God created males and females in God's image, to be in relationship with God and with one another. We can celebrate and appreciate our differences as we try to grow closer in our relationships with one another.

Main Ideas

Men and women. Guys and girls. Dudes and babes. Males and females. God created two very different types of human beings. Sometimes their differences result in mutual bewilderment, irritation, or frustration. At best, the differences between males and females complement each other, leading toward understanding, appreciation, and respect, and making for some pretty good friendships, partnerships, and romantic relationships. At worst, gender differences can lead to major misunderstanding and miscommunication, insensitivity, stereotyping, and prejudice.

Relationships are important to Christians. Within relationships we experience God's love as well as share it with others, so it's important to know how to nurture our relationships. One way to do that is to be aware of our gender differences. Men and women generally differ in how they communicate, process information, perceive things, and relate one-on-one and socially. Understanding these differences—as well as our different hopes, fears, needs, and life experiences—helps Christian men and women encourage and help each other. Recognizing and appreciating our differences affirms who God created us to be and points to our need to be in relationship with each other. We can learn a lot from each other as we seek to grow—not just as men and women of God, but as Christian brothers and sisters in the faith community.

Read, Research, Reflect
Genesis 1:27-28a, 31; 2:18, 20-25

Read the Scripture and additional info in your *Synago* Notebook. Make notes on the following:

- Who is "speaking" or telling the story in each passage? Who is the intended audience? What is the context? (What do you think the situation is? What's happening before and after each passage?)
- Pray about and reflect on the readings. What do they say to you?

Memorize

So God created humankind in his image, in the image of God he created them; male and female he created them. (Genesis 1:27, NRSV)

Prepare

- Note your own answers to each question.
- Decide how you will close. (See page 28.)
- Get supplies.

Session Plan

Opening

5 minutes

Welcome/Announcements/Purpose Statement/Prayer

Warm-Up

10 minutes

Have the group brainstorm a list of "typical" characteristics of guys and a list of "typical" characteristics of girls. Write these on a large sheet of paper. Depending on the makeup and size of your group, you could break into smaller groups for this activity and form coed groups or have a guys' group and a girls' group. Make sure that each group has pen and paper. Give the group(s) 3–5 minutes to brainstorm, then share the lists. Watch the clock!

Topic Talk

20 minutes

1. Even though there are a lot of differences between males and females, what would you say are three primary, fundamental differences—aside from the obvious physical differences?

2. What differences do you think cause the most difficulty in guys and girls relating to each other?

3. a. Girls: What do you think guys misunderstand the most about girls? What advice would you give them to help them understand and relate to girls better?
   b. Guys: What do you think girls misunderstand the most about guys? What advice would you give them to help them understand and relate to guys better?

4. a. Girls: What characteristics or traits about guys do you appreciate most?
   b. Guys: What characteristics or traits about girls do you appreciate most?

Word Search   Genesis 1:27-28a, 31; 2:18, 20-25

15 minutes

Have a volunteer read Genesis 1:27-28a, 31 aloud.

1. What do you think it means that both males and females were created in God's image?

2. What was God's response to creating men and women? How did God feel about it?

Have a volunteer read Genesis 2:18, 20-25 aloud. (This comes from the second of two creation stories in Genesis.)

3. What is significant about the way the woman in this story was created? What does that say about how her relationship to the man was different from his relationship with other living things?

Supplies: Paper for Warm-Up, pencils or pens, *Synago* Notebook for each person who doesn't have one (or Bibles or copies of the Bible readings and note cards)

* *Questions with an * should be answered by everyone.*

When Boy Meets Girl

Reread verse 25 aloud.

4. How would you describe the type of relationship God originally wanted for man and woman?

R&R—Reflect and Respond   **15 minutes**

1. Why do you think these verses on the creation of man and woman are in the Bible? What do they tell us about men and women? What do they tell us about God?

2. Men and women were created physically different in order to reproduce. But why do you think God created men and women to be such different types of people?

3. Without saying anything, think about the feelings and attitudes you have toward the opposite sex. How do you act toward them as friends or romantic interests? (Leader: Allow group members a moment to think about this.) Now, if you feel comfortable, talk about how your attitudes, feelings, and actions toward members of the opposite sex would change if you thought of them first as a Christian brother or sister? (For example, how would this perspective affect how and whom you date?)

Read aloud, or restate in your own words.

Wrap-Up   **2 minutes**

Relationships are important to Christians. Within relationships, we experience God's love as well as share it with others, so it's important to know how to nurture our relationships. One way to do that is to be aware of our gender differences. Men and women generally differ in how they communicate, process information, perceive things, and relate one-on-one and socially.

Understanding those differences, as well as our different hopes, fears, needs, and life experiences, helps Christian men and women encourage and help each other. Recognizing and appreciating our differences affirm who God created us to be and point to our need to be in relationship with each other. We can learn a lot from each other as we seek to grow—not just as men and women of God, but as Christian brothers and sisters in the faith community.

Celebrations and Concerns   **5 minutes**

Invite group members to share celebrations and concerns.

Closing Prayer   **5 minutes**

How Do You Score in Love?

Life Issue

How to judge if a relationship is good or bad

Faith Connection

Love should be at the core of any relationship that a Christian is in. This holds true for romantic relationships, too, where love is more than warm, gushy feelings, but is expressed in kindness and caring.

Main Ideas

Have you ever been in love? What is being in love? How do you know whether you're in love or whether someone really loves you? Are you looking for a soul mate? Do you think that there's only one special person in the world for you? Or do you think that it's possible to have more than one true-love relationship in your life? Do you believe in love at first sight? Or do you think that falling in love with someone happens over time? And what is the true test of a loving relationship?

As a teenager, you may have a lot of questions about love but find it hard to get answers that satisfy you. With so many couples splitting up nowadays, it's difficult to find real-life examples of loving, committed relationships—people who could answer some of your questions. Most of the information you get about love may come from the media—movies, TV, magazines, music—where love seems to be defined as romance, passion, and sexuality. But when you get into a relationship yourself, you'll find that that kind of love can fizzle pretty quickly. It can leave you feeling empty and unfulfilled—like there must be something more.

Well, there is. But you find it in the love that comes from God—love that is kind, patient, and understanding; love that puts the other person's well-being first; love that is deep, not shallow, because it focuses on the whole relationship, not just the physical. So how can you tell whether you're in a truly loving relationship? If both persons want the best for each other; care about each other; are kind and respectful to each other; have compassion for each other; are forgiving, encouraging, and patient. Those are the marks of real love, as described in the Bible; and they guide Christians, not just in romantic relationships, but in all relationships.

Read, Research, Reflect

1 Corinthians 13:4-7

Read the Scripture and additional info in your *Synago* Notebook. Make notes on the following:

- Who is "speaking" or telling the story in the passage? Who is the intended audience? What is the context? (What do you think the situation is? What's happening before and after the passage? Look especially at chapters 12 and 14.)
- Pray about and reflect on the reading. What does it say to you?

Memorize

Love is patient; love is kind; love is not envious or boastful or arrogant or rude. It does not insist on its own way; it is not irritable or resentful.
(1 Corinthians 13:4-5, NRSV)

Prepare

- Note your own answers to each question.
- Decide what type of prayer you will use for the closing. (See page 28.)
- Get supplies.

Session Plan

* Questions with an * should be answered by everyone.

Opening

5 minutes

Welcome/Announcements/Purpose Statement/Prayer

Warm-Up

10 minutes

Imagine that your group is filling in as an advice columnist for a teen magazine. How would you answer these questions?

Dear Ally,
My boyfriend and I have been together for six months. We are very much in love. Lately, however, he's been spending more time with his buds than with me. He says that he loves me, but I feel jealous of the time he's with his friends. I want to spend all of my time with him. Am I the only one who's really in love?—Confused

Dear Ally,
I hope that you can help me with this problem. All last summer I wanted to go out with this girl, and she wouldn't have anything to do with me. I was crazy about her. I finally got her to go out with me when school started, and it was like we were meant for each other. I have never been so close to anyone before, and I know she feels the same way. But lately, even though I still love her, I can't stop thinking about her best friend, who has been my lab partner in chemistry. We've really gotten close, too. Can you be in love with two people at the same time? Am I really in love with either of them? Help! I've got to ask somebody to the prom!—Tangled Up

Dear Ally,
I'm dating the hottest guy at school. He's fun to be around and really popular; but when it's just the two of us together, it can be disappointing. We're really attracted to each other physically; but otherwise, he doesn't seem very interested in me. I admit that I don't share any of his interests either. He's pretty full of himself, too, and only does nice things for me when he gets something out of it. If I hang in this relationship a little longer and try harder, do you think that things may change? Does love just take time? Do I want too much in a relationship?—Wasting My Time?

Topic Talk

15 minutes

1. Two people tell you that they are in love and ask your advice about their relationship. What do you tell them if they are both 12 years old? 14 years old? 18 years old? Is there a way to determine whether two people are really in love, regardless of their age?

2. What or who has taught you the most about what it means to be in love? What has influenced your own ideas about what being in a loving relationship is all about?*

3. When you think about being in a loving relationship with someone, what expectations do you have of yourself and of the other person?

Word Search 1 Corinthians 13:4–7 15 minutes

1. This Bible passage describes love and is often read at weddings. It is about love in any relationship, but we can use it to see if our ideas about romantic love measure up. As the passage is read aloud, think about past relationships or the one you are in now.

Have a volunteer read aloud two translations of the passage, using the Synago Notebook or copies of *The Message* and the NRSV Bible.

2. How can you know for sure that someone loves you, according to these verses?

3. Do you agree with this description of love? What would you change or add?

4. How does this description differ from our culture's portrayal of love?

R&R—Reflect and Respond 15 minutes

1. Is this kind of love possible? Is it worth waiting for or working toward? Should we expect less? Should we settle for something else?

2. How are your experiences of love or your ideas about being in love similar to or different from the love described in the Bible reading?

Read aloud, or restate in your own words, to the group.

3. Name one of the characteristics of love from the Bible reading that's an area you personally need to work on in your current or future love life.*

Wrap-Up 2 minutes

With so many couples splitting up, it's hard to find real-life examples of loving, committed relationships—people who can provide some answers to your questions. A lot of the information we get about love comes from the media—movies, TV, magazines, music—where love seems defined by romance, passion, and sex. But when you get in a relationship yourself, you'll find that that kind of love can fizzle pretty quickly. It can leave you feeling empty and unfulfilled—like there must be something more.

Well, there is. But you find it in the love that comes from God—love that is kind, patient, and understanding; love that puts the other person's well-being first; love that is deep, not shallow, because it focuses on the whole relationship, not just the physical. So how can you tell whether you're in a truly loving relationship? If both persons want the best for each other; care about each other; are kind and respectful to each other; have compassion for each other; are forgiving, encouraging, and patient. Those are the marks of real love, as described in the Bible; and they guide Christians, not just in romantic relationships, but in all relationships.

Celebrations and Concerns 15 minutes

Invite group members to share celebrations and concerns. Ask them to tell if they are in a relationship, just starting one, trying to end one, or getting over one. (Leader: Emphasize confidentiality.)

Closing Prayer 5 minutes

Starting with the leader, go around the circle. Each person prays aloud for the person on his or her left and for any relationship he or she may have shared. If the person praying prefers, it's OK just to say the person's name as a prayer.

How Do You Score in Love?

Life Issue

Sexual intimacy

Faith Connection

Believing that God's Holy Spirit lives within them and that they belong to God, Christians choose to honor God with their bodies as they make decisions about sexual intimacy.

Memorize

God paid a great price for you. So use your body to honor God. (1 Corinthians 5:20, CEV)

Main Ideas

What was God thinking? God created our bodies to serve as a temple, or dwelling place, for the Holy Spirit. Did God not foresee any conflict or difficulty with that when God also wired us to be sexual beings? When the body chemistry is right between you and someone else, you feel excited and alive, along with lots of other feelings as well. To think of your body as the temple of God's Spirit can cool things off pretty quickly. Is it possible to honor God with your body and have sexual desires too?

Being physically close to someone helps you express feelings of affection and love. Sexual intimacy is a gift and a blessing in a committed relationship (such as intercourse in marriage), but we can harm ourselves and others if we seek sexual intimacy and gratification as ends in themselves. We dishonor God when we use or abuse our bodies—and the bodies of others—for sexual satisfaction and as a means to be controlling in a relationship.

Our sex-obsessed society values physical attractiveness and sexuality more than kindness, compassion, respect, honesty, and purity. We get messages from our culture (maybe even from our peers) that certain levels of physical intimacy are expected as a relationship "progresses"; that intimate physical activity, such as oral sex or intercourse, is an expression (or proof) of love and commitment; and that even sex just for the fun of it is OK, as long as it's practiced "safely."

Talk about misinformation! If we're honest with ourselves, no matter how gratifying and pleasurable physical intimacy is, our deepest needs are to grow closer emotionally and spiritually with someone—to be with someone interested in us as persons, someone who accepts and loves us unconditionally. When we focus on the physical part of a relationship, however, we're unlikely to have those deeper needs met. When we make faithful choices about sexual intimacy, not only do we honor God, we discover that the gift of sexual intimacy is at its best in a relationship built on love—mutual caring, friendship, respect—and commitment.

Prepare

- Note your own answers to the questions.
- Decide how you'll close in prayer. (See page 28.)
- Get supplies. Don't forget the candy!

Read, Research, Reflect　　　　　　　　1 Corinthians 6:12-20

Read the Scripture and additional info in your *Synago* Notebook. Make notes on the following:

- Who is "speaking" or telling the story in the passage? Who is the intended audience? What is the context? (What do you think the situation is? What's happening before and after the passage?)
- Pray about and reflect on the reading. What does it say to you?

Session Plan

Supplies: An individually wrapped chocolate candy or other piece of candy, Synago Notebook for each person, pencils or pens, Bibles or copies of the Bible readings and note cards for those who don't have a Synago Notebook

Opening

5 minutes

Welcome/Announcements/Purpose Statement/Prayer

Warm-Up

5 minutes

See who can come up with the best pick-up line or "flirtatious conversation starter."* (Give the winner a piece of candy.)

Topic Talk

15 minutes

1. What things do you think have the greatest influence on teenagers' opinions, attitudes, and behaviors when it comes to sexual intimacy in relationships? (Examples: media, parents, friends, faith, other) In what ways?

2. What factors have had the greatest influence on your personal opinions and attitudes about physical intimacy in relationships?*

3. Do girls and guys have different expectations and desires when it comes to physical intimacy in relationships? Explain.

Word Search **1 Corinthians 6:12-20**   **20 minutes**

Introduce the reading by revealing some information about the writer, Paul, and the context in which he wrote the passage. Have volunteers read 1 Corinthians 6:12-20 aloud. Then reread verses 12-14 aloud before answering the following questions:

1. a. Looking at verse 12, what are some ways in which sexual intimacy would not be good for us?
   b. What kind of power could it have over us?

2. How would you describe the attitude of the people Paul quotes in verses 12 and 13? Do you know anybody like that?

Have a volunteer reread verses 15-17 aloud.

3. a. How can the things we do with our physical bodies—like eating or sexual activity—affect our spiritual selves?
   b. Why do you think God's interest in how we use our bodies extends beyond our lives here on earth?

4. What do these verses say about the spiritual nature of sexual intercourse?

Have a volunteer reread verses 18-20 aloud.

5. How do you think Paul would define *sexual immorality*?

* Questions with an * should be answered by everyone.

Getting Physical

6. What do you think Paul means when he says that sexual immorality "is a sin against your own body in a way that no other sin is"? (The answer is in verse 19.)

7. In verses 19-20, what reasons does Paul give for why we should honor God with our bodies?

R&R—Reflect and Respond

20 minutes

1. When it comes to being sexually active, many people will say, as Paul quoted in his letter, " 'We can do anything we want to' " (verse 12). As a Christian, how would you respond to friends who say that about their decisions to be sexually active?

2. What can be some of the negative fallout or consequences when you are sexually active, or commit sexual sin, in a relationship? Include physical, emotional, and spiritual consequences.

3 If teenagers thought of their bodies as sacred places, and if they knew how much God loved them and sacrificed for them (God's own Son), how do you think their attitudes and behaviors about their bodies and the bodies of others might change?

Read aloud, or restate in your own words.

Wrap-Up

2 minutes

If we're honest with ourselves, no matter how gratifying and pleasurable physical intimacy is, our deepest needs are to grow closer emotionally and spiritually with someone—to be with someone interested in us as a person, someone who accepts and loves us unconditionally. When we focus on the physical part of a relationship, however, we're unlikely to have those deeper needs met.

If you're feeling that you've hurt yourself and others and dishonored God with sexually immoral thoughts and actions, God offers you forgiveness, hope, encouragement, and the strength and guidance of the Holy Spirit, who dwells in you.

When we make faithful choices about sexual intimacy, not only do we honor God, we experience sexual intimacy at its best in a relationship built on love—mutual caring, friendship, respect—and commitment.

Celebrations and Concerns

5 minutes

Invite group members to share celebrations and concerns.

Closing Prayer

5 minutes

Prayer Power

Life Issue

Understanding the power and effects of prayer

Faith Connection

Christians can pray with hope and confidence that God hears and answers our prayers.

Main Ideas

You've probably heard prayer described as talking to God. But think about it—talking to *God*—the Creator of the universe and all that's in it, Spirit of incomprehensible love and grace and truth, a Living Force of good and holiness at work in the world to bring about justice and peace. And you have a personal connection, whenever and wherever you feel like "logging on."

According to the Scriptures, not only are we able to communicate with God through prayer, but our God desires and encourages that communication. God wants us to come to God in prayer like a child comes to a parent, telling it like it is, whether we're whiny or thankful, and asking for the things we want and need. Like a parent, what means most to God is that we simply come, whether it is to converse, ask, plead, or unload. Coming to God in prayer lets God know we're in the relationship, trusting and depending or just honestly seeking.

Jesus Christ taught that God hears and responds to our prayers. He also compared God to earthly parents who always want to provide for their children. Just as children are sometimes awkward in asking for what they want, so we may feel awkward talking to God. But that's OK. You don't have to pray eloquently and say "thee" and "thou" and "O, Lord" a lot for God to tune in to you. Because God's Spirit dwells in us, in kind of a strange and mysterious way, our words aren't even necessary. God listens with "spiritual ears," knowing exactly what we want and need.

God is near you when you pray; God knows what you are praying for and what you need; God responds to each of your prayers. So, what are you waiting for? Pray. Pray. Pray. It is the most powerful spiritual tool you have at your disposal. Prayer changes lives. Prayer can change your life. Prayer can change the world. Pray and see.

Read, Research, Reflect — Deuteronomy 4:7; Matthew 7:7-8; Romans 8:26

Read the Scripture and additional info in your *Synago* Notebook. Make notes on the following:

- Who is "speaking" or telling the story in each passage? Who is the intended audience? What is the context? (What do you think the situation is? What's happening before and after each passage?)
- Pray about and reflect on the readings. What do they say to you?

Memorize

"Ask, and you will receive. Search, and you will find. Knock, and the door will be opened for you."
(Matthew 7:7, CEV)

Prepare

- Note your own answers to each question.
- Review the Closing Prayer, which uses the ACTS of prayer model so that you'll feel comfortable with it.
- Get supplies, particularly newspaper articles about persons and situations in your community or the world to pray for as "Special Requests" in the Closing Prayer.

Supplies: Clip several newspaper articles about persons or situations in your community or state or in the world for whom group members can choose to pray in the Closing Prayer. You may want to include clippings from the obituary section of the newspaper so that group members can pray for families and friends who have recently lost loved ones. Have on hand a *Synago* Notebook for each person, pencils or pens, Bibles or copies of the Bible readings, and note cards for those who don't have a *Synago* Notebook.

* Questions with an * should be answered by everyone.

Opening　　　　　　　　　**5 minutes**

Welcome/Announcements/Purpose Statement/Prayer

Warm-Up　　　　　　　　　**5 minutes**

How would you complete the following statement? Why?*
If praying is like placing a phone call to God, then

a. most of my calls are 911　　　c. most of my calls get disconnected
b. most of my calls are 411　　　d. most of my calls don't get returned
e. I'm glad I don't have to pay the phone bill, because it is huge.

Topic Talk　　　　　　　　**15 minutes**

1. How would you explain prayer to someone who didn't know what it was?*

2. What has had the most influence in shaping your own understanding and practice of prayer?*

3. Do you believe that God answers prayer? That prayer changes things? Why or why not?

4. If you can, tell a personal experience of having a prayer answered or seemingly not answered. How has it affected your beliefs about prayer? Your practice of prayer?

Word Search　　Deuteronomy 4:7; Matthew 7:7-8; Romans 8:26　　**15 minutes**

Ask volunteers to read the Bible passages aloud.

1. In the first reading, the "other nations" worshiped a variety of gods. With that in mind, what do we learn about God's activity in the lives of the Hebrew people and our lives?

2. In the reading from Matthew, what does Jesus teach about prayer, and what effect should it have on how a Christian prays and what he or she prays for?

3. What do you think the "door" might refer to? (perhaps a challenge, opportunity, direction)

Reread Romans 8:26 aloud.

4. Why don't we need to have the right words in order to pray to God?

R&R—Reflect and Respond　　　　　　**15 minutes**

1. a. Why is it that some people don't feel close to God when they pray, and some haven't experienced God answering their prayers?
   b. What encouragement would you offer someone with these experiences?

2. Which word, phrase, or sentence from one of the verses that we've read speaks to where you are in your prayer life?* Explain why.

3. Choose one thing that you will pray for on a daily basis—for yourself, for someone else, or for the world at large—even though it may seem impossible to be answered.* (Write this in your *Synago* Notebook or on a note card to keep.)

Wrap-Up

2 minutes

According to the Scriptures, not only are we able to communicate with God through prayer, but our God desires and encourages that communication. God wants us to come to God in prayer like a child comes to a parent, telling it like it is, whether we're whiny or thankful, and asking for the things we want and need. Like a parent, what means most to God is that we simply come, whether it is to converse, ask, plead, or unload. Coming to God in prayer lets God know we're in the relationship, trusting and depending or just honestly seeking.

Jesus Christ taught that God hears and responds to our prayers. He also compared God to earthly parents who always want to provide for their children. Just as children are sometimes awkward in asking for what they want, so we may feel awkward talking to God. But that's OK. You don't have to pray eloquently and say "thee" and "thou" and "O, Lord" a lot for God to tune in to you. Because God's Spirit dwells in us, in kind of a strange and mysterious way, our words aren't even necessary. God listens with "spiritual ears," knowing exactly what we want and need.

God is near you when you pray; God knows what you are praying for and what you need; God responds to each of your prayers. So, what are you waiting for? Pray. Pray. Pray. It is the most powerful spiritual tool you have at your disposal. Prayer changes lives. Prayer can change your life. Prayer can change the world. Pray and see.

Read aloud, or restate in your own words, to the group.

Celebrations and Concerns

10 minutes

Ask group members to share celebrations and concerns. Hand out newspaper clippings or obituary sections that inform group members of people and situations in your community and in the world that need prayer. Ask for volunteers to pray for some of these needs during the Special Requests time of the Closing Prayer.

Closing Prayer

10 minutes

Review the ACTS method of praying (see page 38), which can be done privately or in group prayer:

Ask group members to hold hands, and invite them to use the ACTS of prayer. Starting with adoration (*A*), take turns around the circle with group members saying a phrase or sentence complimenting God's character or deeds. Then have group members take turns confessing (*C*) one thing for which they desire God's forgiveness. This could be a word or phrase. Take turns again thanking (*T*) God. Take turns around the circle a final time, with group members offering a prayer request (*S,* for special requests) for themselves or others.

Life Issue

The concept of Sabbath

Faith Connection

When Christians observe the Sabbath, they take a "time out" from their regular routine and responsibilities to rest the body and refresh the soul. By keeping Sabbath, Christians honor God and nurture their identity as a community of God's children.

Main Ideas

If you were playing a team sport, acting in a drama group, or playing in a band, you wouldn't dream of participating the whole time without taking any kind of a break. Why? Because you need the rest, as well as the time to assess how things are and to refocus on what's next.

Being a Christian requires taking regular time outs, too. It's called Sabbath time, and many Christians take that time out on Sunday. Regular weekly activity is put on hold so that Christians can physically rest and nurture their spiritual lives. Serving others, living the Christian life as best you can, trying to be a witness to others—well, it can all be very draining. We need time when we check ourselves out of the action—to realize that God is in control and that things can go on without us for a while. We also need to take time out to "reboot" ourselves spiritually. We can get that much-needed boost by going to church, where we can learn and worship with other believers.

Coming together as a faith family to worship our God is also important in maintaining our identity, both as individual Christians and as a Christian people. When we attend a service of worship, we affirm our identity as God's children, as followers of Jesus Christ, and as brothers and sisters to one another. Observing the Sabbath honors God as we offer praise, thanksgiving, confession, and prayers for ourselves and our world. When we set aside regular Sabbath time, we emerge rested, refreshed, refocused, and reminded of whose we are and the real work ahead of us.

Read, Research, Reflect
Exodus 20:8-11; Psalm 149:1-4

Read the Scripture and additional info in your *Synago* Notebook. Make notes on the following:

- Who is "speaking" or telling the story in each passage? Who is the intended audience? What is the context? (What do you think the situation is? What's happening before and after each passage?)
- Pray about and reflect on the readings. What do they say to you?

Memorize

*Remember the sabbath day, and keep it holy."
(Exodus 20:8, NRSV)*

Prepare

- Note your own answers to each question.
- Decide how you will close in prayer, if you don't use the suggested closing. (See page 28.)
- Get supplies. Don't forget what you need for the friendship bracelets.

Session Plan

Supplies: *Synago* Notebook for each person who doesn't have one (or Bibles or copies of the Bible readings and note cards); pencils or pens

Opening   5 minutes

Welcome/Announcements/Purpose Statement/Prayer

Warm-Up   10 minutes

If you went to church as a child, tell about an early memory you have of attending church. If you didn't go to a church when you were young, either tell about an experience you have had at a church or an impression of what you think being in a worship service would be like.*

Topic Talk   15 minutes

1. Briefly describe how you spend a typical Sunday.*

2. Traditionally, Christians have observed Sabbath—a day of rest and worship—on Sunday. Jewish people observe Sabbath from sundown on Friday through sundown on Saturday. What obstacles to observing Sabbath do we face in our culture and society? (school and sports activities held on Sundays, jobs with Sunday hours, sleeping instead of going to worship, friends or family who don't go to church)

* Questions with an * should be answered by everyone.

Word Search   Exodus 20:8-11; Psalm 149:1-4   15 minutes

Ask a volunteer to read Exodus 20:8-11 aloud.

1. What specific commands does God give the Hebrew people about a Sabbath day? Why? (Leader: Don't let group members get side-tracked as to the length of time it took God to create the earth. Keep the focus on how God intentionally stopped work to rest.)

Have another volunteer read Psalm 149:1-4 aloud.

2. What is the mood or tone of this reading?

3. How does coming together in worship help the Hebrew people maintain their identity?

4. According to verse 4, how does our praise and worship affect God?

R&R Reflect and Respond   20 minutes

1. What similarities are there between taking a time out or break during a game, practice, rehearsal, or performance and observing the Sabbath? (Both give body and mind a rest and a time to reflect and refocus. They reinforce personal identity as well as belonging to something bigger than yourself and encourage humility. They are opportunities to connect with and support "teammates" or fellow believers. They keep the common goal or focus in front of you. They usually happen at a scheduled time, so they are part of a balanced routine.)

Time Out

2. Think about Jesus and all of the things he did in his ministry—teaching, healing, spending time with people, and so forth. How do you think he observed the Sabbath and took time out?

3. Do you have meaningful Sabbath time in your life? Why, or why not? What is one thing you could do to better meet your needs for rest and reflection?*

Wrap-Up

2 minutes

Being a Christian requires taking regular time outs, too. It's called Sabbath time, and many Christians take that time out on Sunday. Regular weekly activity is put on hold so that Christians can physically rest and nurture their spiritual lives. Serving others, living the Christian life as best you can, trying to be a witness to others—well, it can all be very draining. We need time when we check ourselves out of the action—to realize that God is in control and that things can go on without us for a while. We also need to take time out to "reboot" ourselves spiritually. We can get that much-needed boost by going to church, where we can learn and worship with other believers.

Coming together as a faith family to worship our God is also important in maintaining our identity, both as individual Christians and as a Christian people. When we attend a service of worship, we affirm our identity as God's children, as followers of Jesus Christ, and as brothers and sisters to one another. Observing the Sabbath honors God as we offer praise, thanksgiving, confession, and prayers for ourselves and our world. When we set aside regular Sabbath time, we emerge rested, refreshed, refocused, and reminded of whose we are and the real work ahead of us.

Read aloud, or restate in your own words.

Celebrations and Concerns

5 minutes

Ask group members to share celebrations and concerns. Invite group members who are not regularly attending church to go with you or another group member to an upcoming worship experience.

Closing Prayer

5 minutes

Sweet Temptations: Materialism — Leader Prep

Life Issue

Materialism

Faith Connection

Christians, particularly those in industrialized countries, must make faithful lifestyle choices about wealth and possessions. Are we attached more to Christ or to our stuff?

Main Ideas

Most of us consider ourselves to be decent people. We don't do anything really bad—no major sinning, such as murder or robbery. We are regulars at our church, youth group, or small group. We're cruising along, feeling OK about ourselves. But it's precisely when we have those comfortable feelings that we need to check out things in our lives that could be distracting or pulling us away from God. These are sweet temptations—seemingly harmless attitudes and activities that deliver lots of gratification—yet they gently chip away at our faith commitment. We'll take a look at materialism, revenge, and deceit. Are you squirming yet?

Materialism is when having things is one of the most important values in your life. How much is too much? You have to answer that for yourself. You have to make an honest assessment of how much you have; what you spend money on; how much money you spend; and whether you are willing to share, give away, or be without the things you have. In other words, what could you live without?

Jesus Christ understood the power that possessions can have on us. It was a favorite topic of his. He said clearly that if you want the blessings that his followers receive (blessings in this life and the life to come) your primary attachment must be to him—not to a comfortable lifestyle, not to stuff, not to dreams of wealth and status. Jesus knew what people who have it all can tell you—that the temporary enjoyment of possessions doesn't take away pain, heartache, fear, uncertainty, emptiness, or insecurity. Ironically, wealth may actually contribute to those negative experiences and doesn't give you a strong sense of purpose in life either.

Attach yourself to Christ. Focus on your relationship to him and follow his lead. Don't let materialism rob you of experiencing the unending and unfading joy of the abundant, truly satisfying life that he can provide.

Read, Research, Reflect   Luke 18:18-30

Read the Scripture and additional info in your *Synago* Notebook. Make notes on the following:

- Who is "speaking" or telling the story in each passage? Who is the intended audience? What is the context? (What do you think the situation is? What's happening before and after each passage?)
- Pray about and reflect on the readings. What do they say to you?

Memorize

"You can be sure that anyone who gives up home or wife or brothers or family or children because of God's kingdom, will be given much more in this life. And in the future world they will have eternal life." (Luke 18:29-30, CEV)

Prepare

- Note your own answers to the session questions.
- Decide how you'll close in prayer. (See page 28.)
- Get supplies.

Sweet Temptations: Materialism

Session Plan

Supplies: *Synago* Notebook for each person, pencils or pens, Bibles or copies of the Bible readings and note cards for those who don't have a *Synago* Notebook

* Questions with an * should be answered by everyone.

Opening — 5 minutes

Welcome/Announcements/Purpose Statement/Prayer

Warm-Up — 5 minutes

If you had a million dollars, what would you do with it?*

Topic Talk — 20 minutes

1. Think of all the things you currently own. If you could keep only one of them, what would it be?*

2. What does it mean to be materialistic?

3. On a scale of 1 to 10, with 10 being extremely materialistic, rate how materialistic the average teenager at your school is. On what do you base that rating?

4. Briefly describe the personal values of the following in terms of money and possessions. How are these values lived out?*

    a. your parent(s)   b. you

5. What or who has had the greatest influence on shaping your current values and behavior regarding wealth and possessions?*

Word Search — Luke 18:18-30 — 20 minutes

Have a volunteer read Luke 18:18-27 aloud.

1. Describe the wealthy man in this reading. What type of person do you think he was? For what was he really searching?

2. What does Jesus mean by "God's kingdom"?

3. How do you think Jesus felt towards the wealthy man? Why do you think that?

Have a volunteer read Luke 18:28-30 aloud.

4. What does Jesus say is the reward for those who are willing to give up the most important things in their lives in order to follow Christ?

R&R—Reflect and Respond — 20 minutes

1. Do you think Jesus is saying that we have to leave our families, give away all our possessions to the poor, and be missionaries or work in a church or service organization in order to live out our commitment to him? What do you think Jesus is trying to teach us about what it means to follow him? Do you find truth in that?

2. Reflect on your life and the things you value most (as measured by your time investment, how much you have, and how difficult it would be to part with those things). What is one area of your life where you are materialistic and need to emotionally or physically "give it away" or sacrifice it to follow Christ more faithfully?*

Wrap-Up 2 minutes

Materialism is when having things is one of the most important values in your life. How much is too much? You have to answer that for yourself. You have to make an honest assessment of how much you have; what you spend money on; how much money you spend; and whether you are willing to share, give away, or be without the things you have. In other words, what could you live without?

Jesus Christ understood the power that possessions can have on us. It was a favorite topic of his. He said clearly that if you want the blessings that his followers receive (blessings in this life and the life to come) your primary attachment must be to him—not to a comfortable lifestyle, not to stuff, not to dreams of wealth and status. Jesus knew what people who have it all can tell you—that the temporary enjoyment of possessions doesn't take away pain, heartache, fear, uncertainty, emptiness, or insecurity. Ironically, wealth may actually contribute to those negative experiences and doesn't give you a strong sense of purpose in life either.

Attach yourself to Christ. Focus on your relationship to him and follow his lead. Don't let materialism rob you of experiencing the unending and unfading joy of the abundant, truly satisfying life that he can provide.

Read aloud, or restate in your own words.

Celebrations and Concerns   10 minutes

Invite group members to share celebrations and concerns for others to pray for during the week.

Closing Prayer   5 minutes

Sweet Temptations: Revenge — Leader Prep

Life Issue

Wanting to get back at someone

Faith Connection

To follow Christ means answering to a higher call (God's call) than our own personal sense or society's sense of fairness. What makes Christians stand out from the crowd is choosing not to get revenge on people who don't like us, mistreat us, or have it in for us.

Main Ideas

"I don't get mad—I get even." Have you ever said that or felt that way? There's an attitude in our society, even among our peers, that taking revenge on someone who has insulted you or mistreated you, or who just seems to have it in for you is not only acceptable but expected. Nobody blames you for hurting someone if you're just "paying them back" or they "deserve" it.

Well, if you're serious about following Christ and the way you witness to that commitment, this is one temptation you must fight against with all your might. Jesus taught us to "do to others *as you would have them do to you*" (Luke 6:31) not "do to others *because they did it to you.*"

Besides helping you develop humility, poise, and self-control, what is the rationale for choosing to "turn the other cheek" and be forgiving, rather than to get revenge? Why are we supposed to be nice to our enemies? Jesus said that even the worst people are nice to people they like. But Jesus said that as God's children, you are to be like God; and God is gracious, kind, merciful, and loving to everyone whether they are deserving or not.

It is hard to let people insult you or hurt you or take advantage of you. (And it doesn't mean that you should allow someone to physically or emotionally abuse you, without trying to stop him or her. That person needs intervention and help.) Christians are called to love those who mistreat them, rather than to respond with the same mistreatment. To love them means to look past their actions to gain understanding and compassion for them (why do they do what they do?) and to treat them kindly.

To walk away from a fight, to ignore an insult, to repay meanness with kindness—to put your honor aside—is to give all the honor to Jesus Christ, as you follow his example and not the world's.

Read, Research, Reflect — Luke 6:27-36

Read the Scripture and additional info in your *Synago* Notebook. Make notes on the following:

- Who is "speaking" or telling the story in the passage? Who is the intended audience? What is the context? (What do you think the situation is? What's happening before and after the passage?)
- Pray about and reflect on the reading. What does it say to you?

Memorize

"Love your enemies, and be good to everyone who hates you." (Luke 6:27b, CEV)

Prepare

- Note your own answers to the session questions.
- Decide how you'll close in prayer. (See page 28.)
- Get supplies.

Sweet Temptations: Revenge

Supplies: *Synago* Notebook for each person, pencils or pens, Bibles or copies of the Bible readings and note cards for those who don't have a *Synago* Notebook

Opening 5 minutes

Welcome/Announcements/Purpose Statement/Prayer

Warm-Up 5 minutes

Briefly tell about a time when you "got even" with someone or felt like getting even with someone.*

Topic Talk 20 minutes

1. In what ways does our culture encourage or discourage revenge or getting even? Can you give examples?

2. Are some people more inclined to want to get even than others? If yes, why do you think that is?

3. Are there certain situations where it should be acceptable to get revenge? certain situations where it should not be?

4. What would you think of someone who allowed others to insult or mistreat him or her without saying or doing something to get back at them?

Word Search　　Luke 6:27-36 10 minutes

Have a volunteer read Luke 6:27-36 aloud.

1. What is your reaction to Jesus Christ's teaching on how we should treat our enemies? (Agree? Disagree? Think it's a nice idea but not realistic?)

2. Glance over the Bible passage again. Which would be the hardest for you to put into practice?

3. In verses 32 through 36, what are the reasons Jesus gives for repaying enemies with kindness instead of getting revenge?

*Questions with an * should be answered by everyone.*

R&R—Reflect and Respond 25 minutes

1. Think about a time when you tried to get back at someone. What would have been a more Christ-like way to handle that?

2. Do you think "turning the other cheek" includes allowing someone to abuse you—either verbally or physically? Why or why not?

3. Think of someone whom you consider an enemy—someone who doesn't like you, insults you or makes fun of you, tries to get you in trouble, maybe even has physically hurt you. Can you talk about this with the group? (Remind group members of their commitment to confidentiality—"What's said in the group stays in the group.") What is a specific way that you can respond to this person that would honor Christ and show God's love?* (Group members should help answer this.)

Wrap-Up

It is hard to let people insult you or hurt you or take advantage of you. (And it doesn't mean that you should allow someone to physically or emotionally abuse you, without trying to stop him or her. That person needs intervention and help.) Christians are called to love those who mistreat them, rather than to respond with the same mistreatment. To love them means to look past their actions to gain understanding and compassion for them (why do they do what they do?) and to treat them kindly.

To walk away from a fight, to ignore an insult, to repay meanness with kindness—to put your honor aside—is to give all the honor to Jesus Christ, as you follow his example and not the world's.

Celebrations and Concerns

Invite group members to share celebrations and concerns.

Closing Prayer

Remember to pray silently or aloud for those persons whom group members discussed in Question 3 of the R & R time.

Sweet Temptations: Deceit   Leader Prep

Life Issue

Deceiving others

Faith Connection

Jesus Christ placed a high value on truth. He even identified himself with it—"I am the way, the truth, and the life" (John 14:6). A Christian's life, filled and empowered by God's love, is marked by honesty, truthfulness, and integrity.

Main Ideas

Lying is sometimes so tempting. Deceitful words and stories can flow out of our mouths so easily, helping us avoid trouble, get something we want, or just make life smoother. And if the lie or deceit doesn't hurt anybody, what's the big deal, right?

The big deal is that when you are deceitful, you do hurt someone—you. Being deceitful affects your relationship with God and others. Maybe not on a surface level but on a deep-down level. It goes to the core of who you are and what you value. Of course, we're not talking about lying to your best friend so that you can arrange a surprise birthday party for him or her. When your intent in deceiving someone is for personal benefit or to hurt someone else, then it's definitely wrong. For a Christian, in whom God's Spirit of love resides, there is no room for deceit.

It may seem hokey, but it's true—although telling the truth may cost you something in the short run, the payoff comes later, when you experience the rewards and blessings that come from living with integrity and telling the truth in love.

Read, Research, Reflect   Exodus 20:16; Mark 7:20-23; Ephesians 4:15

Read the Scripture and additional info in your *Synago* Notebook. Make notes on the following:

- Who is "speaking" or telling the story in each passage? Who is the intended audience? What is the context? (What do you think the situation is? What's happening before and after each passage?)
- Pray about and reflect on the readings. What do they say to you?

Memorize

Love should always make us tell the truth. Then we will grow in every way and be more like Christ. (Ephesians 4:15, CEV)

Prepare

- Note your own answers to the questions.
- Decide how you'll close in prayer. (See page 28.)
- Get supplies; don't forget the tissues.

Supplies: *Synago* Notebook for each person, pencils or pens, Bibles or copies of the Bible readings and note cards for those who don't have a *Synago* Notebook

Opening   **5 minutes**

Welcome/Announcements/Purpose Statement/Prayer

Warm-Up   **5 minutes**

What is one whopper of a lie that you've told, and what happened?*

Topic Talk   **20 minutes**

1. Is deceiving someone, without actually telling a lie, the same as telling a lie? Why, or why not?

2. Is there a time or situation where it would not be wrong to lie or deceive someone? If yes, what would be the criteria for "acceptable" lying? Give a personal example if you have one.

3. Do you agree or disagree with this statement, and why or why not?
   "Lying is OK as long as no one is hurt by it."

4. Can you tell about a time when you told the truth in a situation where you could have easily lied? What happened? Was it worth it to be honest?

* Questions with an * should be answered by everyone.

Word Search   **Exodus 20:16; Mark 7:20-23; Ephesians 4:15**   **15 minutes**

Have a volunteer read Exodus 20:16 aloud.

1. What type of deceit is this commandment talking about?

2. What do you think is so important about this kind of honesty, that God would include it in the "Big Ten"? How does it benefit God's people?

Have another volunteer read Mark 7:20-23 aloud.

3. From where does Jesus say deceit comes? What does that say about the person who deceives?

4. Why would being deceitful make you "unfit" to worship God?

Have another volunteer read Ephesians 4:15 aloud.

5. What does love have to do with telling the truth?

R&R—Reflect and Respond

1. Think about these Bible readings. Why should honesty be an important practice in a Christian's life?

2. How would you encourage a Christian teenager to be honest when he or she is tempted to lie or be deceitful to avoid taking responsibility for his or her actions?

3. Do you need to be more truthful or honest in your life? In what ways?*

4. Do any of you have any confessions that you feel you'd like to make to the group, to receive God's forgiveness and encouragement from the group? (Leader: Remind everyone of confidentiality. And you may need to go first.)

Wrap-Up

 2 minutes

Lying is sometimes so tempting. Deceitful words and stories can flow out of our mouths so easily, helping us avoid trouble, get something we want, or just make life smoother. And if the lie or deceit doesn't hurt anybody, what's the big deal, right?

The big deal is that when you are deceitful, you do hurt someone—you. Being deceitful affects your relationship with God and others. Maybe not on a surface level but on a deep-down level. It goes to the core of who you are and what you value. Of course, we're not talking about lying to your best friend so that you can arrange a surprise birthday party for him or her. When your intent in deceiving someone is for personal benefit or to hurt someone else, then it's definitely wrong. For a Christian, in whom God's Spirit of love resides, there is no room for deceit.

It may seem hokey, but it's true—although telling the truth may cost you something in the short run, the payoff comes later, when you experience the rewards and blessings that come from living with integrity and telling the truth in love.

Read aloud, or restate in your own words.

Celebrations and Concerns

 10 minutes

Invite group members to share celebrations and concerns.

Closing Prayer

 5 minutes

Pray for guidance and strength to be honest and live with integrity.

Life Issue

Considering the person and mission of Jesus Christ

Faith Connection

Throughout a Christian's life, through times of great faith, great doubt, and ordinary routine, he or she will explore the answer to the question Jesus Christ poses to each of us: "Who do you say I am?"

Main Ideas

Sometimes it's the basic questions that trip us up, that challenge us to sort out thoughts and feelings. It can be like that with questions dealing with faith, such as what we believe and in Whom we believe.

We may admire, and even envy, the confident answer of Peter, one of the twelve disciples, when Jesus asked him, "Who do you say I am?" He responded simply, "You're the Christ, the Messiah." His answer impressed Jesus because, to that point, Jesus hadn't said plainly to his disciples who he was or what his mission was. It wasn't by luck or by accident that Peter answered correctly. It was by revelation and understanding given to him by God's Holy Spirit.

So, what do people today say about Jesus? Many of the same things that they were saying 2000 years ago: "Great teacher and model," "Must be a prophet," "A good friend," "The guy can heal." Some of us who have been Christian all of our lives answer quickly that Jesus is God's Son, the Savior. But do we answer from habit or from personal conviction? Sometimes we struggle with the answer, knowing that a truthful answer would reveal that we're still searching and unsure.

Even though the truth of Christ's identity may be all around us, it comes to us only as God's Spirit reveals it to us. Peter didn't know who Jesus really was when he decided to leave everything behind and follow him. Like Peter, you may need to walk with Jesus, learn about him, trust him, and follow his teachings before you have a personal revelation of who Jesus is—before you can believe in him as your personal Savior. Then you can say with the confidence of Peter, "You are the Messiah."

Read, Research, Reflect
Matthew 1:18-21, 24; 3:1-2, 6, 13-15; 4:23-24; 16:13-17; 28:1-6

Read the Scripture and additional info in your *Synago* Notebook. Make notes on the following:

- Who is "speaking" or telling the story in each passage? Who is the intended audience? What is the context? (What do you think the situation is? What's happening before and after each passage?)
- Pray about and reflect on the readings. What do they say to you?

Memorize

[Jesus] pressed [the disciples], "And how about you? Who do you say I am?" Simon Peter said, "You're the Christ, the Messiah, the Son of the living God."
(Matthew 16:15-16, The Message)

Prepare

- Note your own answers to the questions.
- Decide how you'll close in prayer. (See page 28.)
- Get supplies.

Session Plan

Opening   **5 minutes**

Welcome/Announcements/Purpose Statement/Prayer

Warm-Up   **5 minutes**

Play Twenty Questions: Who Am I? Have one person in the group think of a famous person. Other group members get to ask up to twenty yes or no questions (that's twenty questions for the whole group, not individually) to figure out who the person is.

Topic Talk   **20 minutes**

1. Describe one of the first things you remember hearing or learning about Jesus. Include where and when you first learned it.*

2. How has your knowledge, understanding, or belief about Jesus changed over time?

3. What has had the greatest influence in shaping your current impression, belief, or understanding of Jesus?*

4. Are your beliefs about Jesus "basically similar to" or "significantly different from" that of

   a. your parents?   b. your friends?   c. your church (if you attend one)?

Word Search   **20 minutes**
Matthew 1:18-21, 24; 3:1-2, 6, 13-17; 4:23-24; 16:13-17; 28:1-6

Tell the group that the readings are all from the Book of Matthew and tell about events in Jesus' life that deal with his identity and mission.

Have a volunteer read Matthew 1:18-21, 24 aloud from a Bible.

1. What significant information do you think the writer wants you to know about Jesus?

2. Why do you think the writer thought it was important to include the story of Jesus' birth? Why not just start with when his ministry began?

Have a volunteer read Matthew 3:1-2, 6, 13-17 aloud from the Notebook.

3. What do you find in this reading that is significant about who Jesus was?

Read Matthew 4:23-24 from the Notebook and Matthew 28:1-6 from a Bible.

4. What information in these two readings is most important in understanding who Jesus was and what his mission or purpose was?

Have a volunteer read Matthew 16:13-16 aloud from the Notebook.

Supplies: *Synago* Notebook for each person, pencils or pens, Bibles or copies of the Bible readings and note cards for those who don't have a *Synago* Notebook

* Questions with an * should be answered by everyone.

5. Why do you think Jesus asked his disciples who people thought he was and who they thought he was? Do you think he already knew their answers?

6. What was significant about Peter's understanding of Jesus' identity?

R&R—Reflect and Respond 15 minutes

1. Look over the readings again. Is there one that is especially meaningful to you, in terms of your own beliefs about Jesus? (The readings are about his birth, his baptism, his ministries of teaching about God and healing people, his asking the disciples who people thought he was, and his empty tomb being discovered by the two women.)

2. How would you answer the question, "Who is Jesus?"

3. As honestly as you can, describe your current relationship with Christ.*
   a. It's pretty good and continues to grow
   b. You're struggling and searching. You wish that you had Peter's confidence in knowing Jesus.
   c. You don't think that you really have a relationship with Jesus, but you're interested.
   d. You don't have a relationship. The jury's still out on that one.
   e. Other. Explain if you can.

Wrap-Up 2 minutes

Read aloud, or restate in your own words.

We may admire, and even envy, the confident answer of Peter, one of the twelve disciples, when Jesus asked him, "Who do you say I am?" He responded simply, "You're the Christ, the Messiah." His answer impressed Jesus because, to that point, Jesus hadn't said plainly to his disciples who he was or what his mission was. It wasn't by luck or by accident that Peter answered correctly. It was by revelation and understanding given to him by God's Holy Spirit.

Unlike Peter, some of us have been Christian all of our lives. Sometimes we answer quickly that Jesus is God's Son, the Savior. But do we answer from habit or from personal conviction? Sometimes we struggle with the answer, knowing that a truthful answer would reveal that we're still searching and unsure.

Even though the truth of Christ's identity may be all around us, it comes to us only as God's Spirit reveals it to us. Peter didn't know who Jesus really was when he decided to leave everything behind and follow him. Like Peter, you may need to walk with Jesus, learn about him, trust him, and follow his teachings before you have a personal revelation of who Jesus is—before you can believe in him as your personal Savior. Then you can say with the confidence of Peter, "You are the Messiah."

Celebrations and Concerns 5 minutes

If anyone in the group shared that he or she wants to have a relationship with Jesus Christ, is struggling with or searching for faith, or is considering whether or not to become a Christian, invite group members to pray for him or her. You may want to place your hands on the person's head or shoulders while you pray. Inform your youth minister, pastor, or other appropriate adult of any group member who wants to make or renew a Christian commitment. As time permits, invite group members to share celebrations and concerns.

Closing Prayer 5 minutes

The Parent Trap

Life Issue

Relating to parents

Faith Connection

For Christians, Christ's love is to permeate, shape, and guide every relationship—even our relationships with parents. One of the greatest opportunities for Christian teenagers to witness to their faith is in how they relate to and treat their parents or guardians.

Main Ideas

"Parents—can't live with them; can't live without them." Does this express how you feel sometimes about your parents or guardians? As you and your parents navigate your teenage years, you will encounter rough roads and downright nasty ruts along the way. This bumpy ride is a natural part of your journey toward independence and their journey toward letting you go. It is a trying period, where everyone—both parent and teen—will experience anxiety, uncertainty, frustration, fear, anger, and disappointment. But this is a journey that must be taken—for out of the struggle comes growth, as you and your parents grow into new ways of relating to each other and grow in your understanding and respect for each other.

Your journey may test your faith. Can you be forgiving of, patient with, respectful of, and compassionate toward a parent or guardian? Responsibility goes hand in hand with independence. One of the greatest opportunities to experience God's presence in your life and to witness to your faith is in treating your parents the way Christians are called to treat all people, including the people with whom you live and who really know how to drive you crazy.

God has placed parents in a position of honor within families. Parents are imperfect, sinful, and mistake prone; but we are to respect them and obey them. (Do you know that one of the meanings of the Latin root for *obey* is to listen carefully?) Parents may or may not deserve our respect, but we should respect them out of our devotion and faithfulness to Jesus Christ. Although this honoring is easier for some teenagers than for others, if you follow God's Word, your faithfulness will be rewarded. Pray for your parents and for yourself, and invite God to be present and active in your relationship with them.

Read, Research, Reflect

Exodus 20:12; Ephesians 5:21, 6:1-4; John 19:25-27

Read the Scripture and additional info in your *Synago* Notebook. Make notes on the following:

- Who is "speaking" or telling the story in each passage? Who is the intended audience? What is the context? (What do you think the situation is? What's happening before and after each passage?)
- Pray about and reflect on the readings. What do they say to you?

Memorize

"Honor your father and mother, so that your days may be long in the land that the LORD your God is giving you."
(Exodus 20:12, NRSV)

Prepare

- Note your own answers to the questions.
- Decide how you'll close in prayer. (See page 28.)
- Get supplies. Don't forget the slips of paper.

The Parent Trap

Session Plan

Supplies: Slips of paper for the Closing Prayer, *Synago* Notebook for each person; pencils or pens; Bibles or copies of the Bible readings and note cards for those who don't have a Synago Notebook

Opening

5 minutes

Welcome/Announcements/Purpose Statement/Prayer

Warm-Up

5 minutes

Name a parent or other adult character from a TV show or movie who resembles your parent(s) or guardian(s)?*

* Questions with an * should be answered by everyone.

Topic Talk

20 minutes

1. Briefly describe your parent(s)/guardian(s) to the rest of the group. Give their first names and talk about what they do and what their personalities are like.*

2. Name one thing about your parent(s)/guardian(s) that you admire and one thing that disappoints you.*

3. Give a one-word description of your current relationship with your parent(s)/guardian(s).*

Word Search

20 minutes

Exodus 20:12; Ephesians 5:21; 6:1—4; John 19:25-27

Have volunteers read Exodus 20:12 and Ephesians 5:21 and 6:1-4 aloud.

1. What do these readings teach about how children should treat their parents?

Leader: Be sensitive to the fact that group members' family situations vary. As appropriate, you may want to include the following terms: parents, parent, step-parent, step-parents, guardian or guardians.

2. Why do you think that honoring parents was important enough to be included in the Ten Commandments and in the teachings of the apostle Paul?

Ask another volunteer to read John 19:25-27 aloud.

3. What is significant about this reading? What example does Jesus give us for treating parents? (Leader: One of the last things Jesus did before he died— and while he was hanging on the cross—was to make sure that his mother would be cared for.)

R&R—Reflect and Respond

15 minutes

1. How would following these teachings affect your relationships with your parent(s)/guardian(s)?

2. What specific responsibilities should we have to our parent(s)/guardian(s)? (Examples include being honest to them, respecting their property, taking care of them when they are old.)

3. What is one thing you could try to do to show more honor or respect to your parent(s) or guardian(s)? (Leader: In what ways can the group encourage one another?)*

Wrap-Up

2 minutes

Your journey may test your faith. Can you be forgiving of, patient with, respectful of, and compassionate toward a parent or guardian? Responsibility goes hand in hand with independence. One of the greatest opportunities to experience God's presence in your life and to witness to your faith is in treating your parents the way Christians are called to treat all people, including the people with whom you live and who really know how to drive you crazy.

God has placed parents in a position of honor in families. Even though parents are imperfect, sinful, and make mistakes (like us!), we are to respect them and be obedient to them—that means listening to them, being attentive. They may or may not deserve our respect, but we respect them anyway out of our devotion and faithfulness to Jesus Christ. This honoring is easier for some of us to do than others, but if you try to follow God's Word, your faithfulness will be rewarded.

Let's pray for our parents and for ourselves, and invite God to be present and active in our relationship with them.

Celebrations and Concerns

10 minutes

Ask group members to tell briefly something about their parent(s) or guardian(s) for which they are thankful and for which they need God's help.

Closing Prayer

5 minutes

Ask each group member to write the first name(s) of his or her parent(s) or guardian(s) on a slip of paper. Collect the slips, then pass them out to the group. As group leader, begin the prayer and ask God to forgive, guide, strengthen, and bless the parents of the members of your group. Pray for them by name, starting with you and going around the group, with each person saying the name(s) on his or her slip of paper.

Read aloud, or restate in your own words.

The Parent Trap

I Doubt It

Leader Prep

Life Issue

Having doubts about faith in God or Jesus Christ

Faith Connection

Having doubts about what you believe as a Christian is more a sign of seeking faith than lacking faith. Being honest about our doubts, while trusting God to either reveal answers or enable us to believe without having all the answers, builds a stronger, more mature faith.

Main Ideas

Do you ever have nagging doubts about basic Christian beliefs? For instance, is there a God? Is there a divine purpose for my life? Was Jesus really who he said he was—God's Son—or was he just a nut? Is there a heaven, or do you die and that's it? Did the Resurrection actually happen? Can I believe what's in the Bible?

Even the most faithful Christians struggle with doubts. Faith, at its best, is a tension between belief and doubt. Our belief keeps us going day to day; and during times of pain and uncertainty, our beliefs can help get us through. Our doubt, ironically, keeps us growing in our belief, because doubt keeps us actively thinking about and testing what we believe, rather than accepting without question the beliefs of others.

Don't be afraid to explore and confront your doubts. Bring them to God in prayer and reflection. Seek the wisdom and support of the faith community and Christians you trust and admire. Then you'll be able to claim a faith that is truly your own, a faith that is shaped by your own reason, experience, and understanding of God's Word.

And when those nagging doubts come along, remember that even the disciples had their moments of doubt. Although their doubts frustrated Jesus, he helped them move beyond doubt to belief, encouraging and reminding them that all things are possible through him. With honesty and hope, we can boldly confess to Christ, "We believe; help our unbelief." The record shows that he will.

Read, Research, Reflect

John 20:24-29; Mark 9:17b-27

Read the Scripture and additional info in your *Synago* Notebook. Make notes on the following:

- Who is "speaking" or telling the story in each passage? Who is the intended audience? What is the context? (What do you think the situation is? What's happening before and after each passage?)
- Pray about and reflect on the readings. What do they say to you?

Memorize

"I believe; help my unbelief!" (Mark 9:24b, NRSV)

Prepare

- Note your own answers to the questions.
- Decide how you'll close in prayer. (See page 28.)
- Get supplies.

I Doubt It

Session Plan

Supplies: *Synago* Notebook for each person, pencils or pens, Bibles or copies of the Bible readings and note cards for those who don't have a *Synago* Notebook

Opening   5 minutes

Welcome/Announcements/Purpose Statement/Prayer

Warm-Up   10 minutes

Briefly say something about yourself—either true or false—that no one else in the group would know whether or not it's true. (Examples: "I've hiked the Appalachian Trail," "My favorite food is bacon," "I've been to the hospital emergency room ten times.") After group members respond with "I believe it" or "I doubt it," tell if it's true or false.*

Topic Talk   15 minutes

1. What is one thing related to the Christian faith about which you have doubts (such as a particular Christian belief or Bible story)?* (Leader: Ask whether other group members have had the same doubt. How has it been resolved or answered?)

2. Do you agree or disagree with the following statement? Why, or why not?

"When I start to doubt something that I have believed about the Christian faith or that other Christians believe, it shows that I lack faith and that I am not a strong Christian."

* Questions with an * should be answered by everyone.

3. What are some negative and positive ways that a person's doubts can affect his or her relationship with God?

Word Search   John 20:24-29; Mark 9:17b-27   15 minutes

Ask a volunteer to read John 20:24-29 aloud.

1. What did Thomas need in order to believe that Jesus had risen from the dead and had appeared to the other disciples? Why do you think he couldn't take the other disciples' word for it?

2. How did Jesus respond to Thomas' need to actually see the risen Christ in order to believe? Would you say that Jesus was frustrated, angry, or understanding about Thomas's need for proof? Why? What did Jesus do about Thomas's need for proof?

3. What two types of belief did Jesus recognize and affirm in his response to Thomas? (Leader: Jesus affirmed Thomas's need for proof and personal experience by giving Thomas that proof. Jesus also affirmed those who are able to believe without having evidence and all the answers. Christ responded to both types of believers.)

I Doubt It

Have another volunteer read Mark 9:17b-27 aloud.

4. With whom does Jesus become frustrated? Why?

5. (Leader: Ask group members to listen carefully as you reread the last half of the passage beginning with, "He asked the boy's father. . . .") The boy's father pleads with Jesus that, *if* Jesus can do anything, to "have a heart" and help his son. For which of the following reasons do you think Jesus healed the boy?

    a. Because of the man's faith
    b. Because of the man's doubts
    c. Because of Jesus' compassion and desire to heal
    d. Other

R&R—Reflect and Respond 15 minutes

1. Thinking about your own faith and doubts, with whom do you identify the most—the disciple Thomas or the man with the demon-possessed son? Why?

2. Consider how Jesus responded to Thomas and the man with the sick son when they had doubts. What can you do to stay encouraged when you struggle with doubts?

Wrap-Up 2 minutes

Read aloud, or restate in your own words.

Even the most faithful Christians struggle with doubts. Faith, at its best, is a tension between belief and doubt. Our belief keeps us going day to day; and during times of pain and uncertainty, our beliefs can help get us through. Our doubt, ironically, keeps us growing in our belief, because doubt keeps us actively thinking about and testing what we believe, rather than accepting without question the beliefs of others.

Don't be afraid to explore and confront your doubts. Bring them to God in prayer and reflection. Seek the wisdom and support of the faith community and Christians you trust and admire. Then you'll be able to claim a faith that is truly your own, a faith that is shaped by your own reason, experience, and understanding of God's Word.

And when those nagging doubts come along, remember that even the disciples had their moments of doubt. Although their doubts frustrated Jesus, he helped them move beyond doubt to belief, encouraging and reminding them that all things are possible through him. With honesty and hope, we can boldly confess to Christ, "We believe; help our unbelief." The record shows that he will.

Celebrations and Concerns 5 minutes

Ask group members to share celebrations and concerns.

Closing Prayer 5 minutes

Synago: Calm in the Storm

Life Issue

Dealing with troubling and unsettling situations

Faith Connection

During difficult and trying times, Christians can experience peace, strength, and hope through their faith in Jesus Christ and his presence in their lives.

Main Ideas

"Life is difficult." These were the first words in a best-selling book by M. Scott Peck, called *The Road Less Traveled*, about the challenges of the Christian life. Yes, life is difficult—at some times more than others. Adolescence is one of those times. Life can be turbulent and stormy as you get battered about by the ever-changing emotions, relationships, and circumstances of your life.

Life would be difficult enough if you had to experience only the normal difficulties that come with your changing body and feelings, figuring out who you are and who you want to be, and working toward a more independent relationship with your parents. But many teenagers must also weather the storms of parents' divorce and other broken relationships, poverty, abuse, addiction, loneliness, low self-esteem, apathy, and tragedy. Life, at times, can be painful, scary, and seemingly hopeless, even under the best circumstances.

Having a relationship with Jesus Christ can help you weather the storms of life. Jesus' desire for us is that we make it through those difficult times and not be drowned by them. Knowing Jesus Christ, trusting him, and following his ways can give you direction when you feel lost and the peace and calm you desire when you are anxious, afraid, and overwhelmed. Look for his presence during these times. Ask for his help, and he will pull you out of the waves and get you back in the boat. The storms of life will come and go, but the peace of Christ is yours forever.

Read, Research, Reflect   Matthew 14:22-33; Mark 4:35-41

Read the Scripture and additional info in your *Synago* Notebook. Make notes on the following:

- Who is "speaking" or telling the story in each passage? Who is the intended audience? What is the context? (What do you think the situation is? What's happening before and after each passage?)
- Pray about and reflect on the readings. What do they say to you?

Memorize

When they climbed into the boat, the wind died down. (Matthew 14:32, NIV)

Prepare

- Note your own answers to the questions.
- Decide how you'll close in prayer. (See page 28.)
- Get supplies.

Calm in the Storm

Opening 5 minutes

Welcome/Announcements/Purpose Statement/Prayer

Warm-Up 5 minutes

What is the scariest weather experience you've ever had?* (Examples: hurricane, tornado, snow storm that left your house without power for a week, violent thunderstorm)

Topic Talk 15 minutes

1. What are some things that make life difficult for teenagers? What worries and fears do they have to deal with?

2. What is one thing that scares you or causes you a lot of anxiety?*

3. When you feel worried or overwhelmed by something, how do you deal with it?

Word Search   Matthew 14:22-33; Mark 4:35-41   15 minutes

Ask a volunteer to read Matthew 14:22-33 and Mark 4:35-41 aloud.

1. Describe what happened to the disciples when they were in the boats. Put yourself in their sandals: What would you be thinking and feeling? What would you have done?

2. In the two readings, how did Jesus respond when the disciples cried out in fear?

3. Do you think that Jesus knew what was going to happen and intentionally sent the disciples out in the boats to encounter the storms? If you think that he did, why did he do it?

4. In the Matthew passage, what do you think motivated Peter to get out of the boat and walk toward Jesus? Why did Peter start sinking?

R&R—Reflect and Respond 20 minutes

1. Think about the disciples and what their life must have been like with Jesus. What fears and anxieties—other than storms at sea—do you think they experienced? In what ways do you think Jesus helped calm the disciples and give them peace?

2. In these stories, do you identify more with Peter or the other disciples? Why?*

* Questions with an * should be answered by everyone.

3. Reread Matthew 14:32 ("When they climbed into the boat, the wind died down.") and Mark 4:39. ("He got up, rebuked. . . .") What might the wind and waves represent in our lives? What might the boat represent?

Wrap—Up 2 minutes

Yes, life is difficult—at some times more than others. Adolescence is one of those times. Life can be turbulent and stormy as you get battered about by the ever-changing emotions, relationships, and circumstances of your life.

Life would be difficult enough if you had to experience only the normal difficulties that come with your changing body and feelings, figuring out who you are and who you want to be, and working toward a more independent relationship with your parents. But many teenagers must also weather the storms of parents' divorce and other broken relationships, poverty, abuse, addiction, loneliness, low self-esteem, apathy, and tragedy. Life, at times, can be painful, scary, and seemingly hopeless, even under the best circumstances.

Having a relationship with Jesus Christ can help you weather the storms of life. Jesus' desire for us is that we make it through those difficult times and not be drowned by them. Knowing Jesus Christ, trusting him, and following his ways can give you direction when you feel lost and the peace and calm you desire when you are anxious, afraid, and overwhelmed. Look for his presence during these times. Ask for his help, and he will pull you out of the waves and get you back in the boat. The storms of life will come and go, but the peace of Christ is yours forever.

Read aloud, or restate in your own words.

Celebrations and Concerns 10 minutes

Ask everyone to share one thing that he or she is really worried or troubled about. Then invite group members to share ways that they have experienced Christ's help or peace in difficult situations.

Closing Prayer 5 minutes

Pray for Christ's help and peace to be with those group members who need it in their lives.

Closing Time

Life Issue

What it is like to be in the Christian faith community

Faith Connection

Christianity is a faith lived out in community with other believers, not in personal isolation. In a faith community, such as a church, youth group, or small group, Christians are able to care for and support one another, share their individual abilities and skills, worship, and reach out to others as the body of Christ.

Main Ideas

As the writer of Ecclesiastes said, "For everything there is a season, and a time for every matter under heaven" (Ecclesiastes 3:1, NRSV). In your life together as members of a small group of friends, gathering regularly to learn about and experience Christian community and to encourage one another in your faith journeys, you have experienced many seasons and times.

You have experienced beginnings with the start up of your small group or your coming as a visitor. You have experienced times of fun and laughter, pain and sorrow. You have agreed and disagreed. You have shared and held back. You have been confused, off track, and on target. You have felt awkward; and you have, it is hoped, felt completely yourself. You have comforted, and you received comfort. At times, you wondered where God was in all of this; and at other times, God's presence and love were so strong in your group that it took your breath away.

Now is the time for bringing your group's experience and life together to a close—for now. Reflect on your journey together and with Christ. Celebrate. Encourage. Affirm. Give thanks.

Read, Research, Reflect   Matthew 18:20; Acts 2:42, 44-47; 1 Thessalonians 5:11

Read the Scripture and additional info in your *Synago* Notebook. Make notes on the following:

- Who is "speaking" or telling the story in each passage? Who is the intended audience? What is the context? (What do you think the situation is? What's happening before and after each passage?)
- Pray about and reflect on the readings. What do they say to you?

Memorize

Therefore encourage one another and build up each other, as indeed you are doing.
(1 Thessalonians 5:11, NRSV)

Prepare

- Note your own answers to the questions.
- Get supplies. You'll need sheets of paper—enough for each member to have one. Optional: CD or tape of soft music, CD player or tape player

---

Closing Time

Session Plan

Opening **5 minutes**

Welcome/Announcements/Purpose Statement/Prayer

Warm-Up **5 minutes**

What is your favorite snack or refreshment to have at a small group meeting?*

Topic Talk **10 minutes**

1. Describe your first time in this small group. What do you remember about it? Was it a good experience, a bad experience, or a so-so experience? Did you come as someone's guest?*

2. If being in this small group were your only experience of being in a family or community of Christians, how would you describe Christian community to someone who didn't know what it was?

Word Search **10 minutes**

Matthew 18:20; Acts 2:42, 44-47; 1 Thessalonians 5:11

Ask volunteers to read Matthew 18:20; Acts 2:42, 44-47' 1 Thessalonians 5:11 aloud.

1. According to these readings, what happens when a small group of Christians gathers together?

2. In what ways has this small group been similar to or different from the small groups of the early Christian church?

3. What is it about a Christian small group that an unchurched person or non-Christian might find appealing?

R&R—Reflect and Respond **35 minutes**

Reread 1 Thessalonians 5:11. Then say something like:

"This is what we hope our small group experience has been for you. As a way to close our last meeting together, we're going to write down some words of encouragement and appreciation for one another."

Give each person a sheet of paper and a pencil or pen. Have each person write his or her name on the paper then pass it to the person on his or her right. Tell group members that when they get someone's sheet, they are to take a minute to write something about that person for which they appreciate or are thankful. When they are finished with their comments, they should pass the paper to the person on their right.

Keep passing the papers around until everyone has written something on each person's "Encouraging Words" paper (except his or her own, of course!). Optional: Play some soft music during this time. Collect all of the sheets when they are completed.

Supplies: *Synago* Notebook for each person, pencils or pens, Bibles or copies of the Bible readings and note cards for those who don't have a *Synago* Notebook, sheet of notebook paper for each person for the closing activity. Optional: CD or tape player and a CD or tape of soft music, Christian if possible, or music that encourages reflection.

* Questions with an * should be answered by everyone.

1. What is a special memory you have from our small group experience—funny, sad, meaningful, or inspiring?*

2. In what ways has the *Synago* experience helped you to grow in the Christian faith?*

3. In what ways has it influenced your beliefs or your lifestyle?*

Wrap Up

2 minutes

Read aloud, or restate in your own words.

As the writer of Ecclesiastes said, "For everything there is a season, and a time for every matter under heaven" (Ecclesiastes 3:1, NRSV). In your life together as members of a small group of friends, gathering regularly to learn about and experience Christian community and to encourage one another in your faith journeys, you have experienced many seasons and times.

You have experienced beginnings with the start up of your small group or your coming as a visitor. You have experienced times of fun and laughter, pain and sorrow. You have agreed and disagreed. You have shared and held back. You have been confused, off track, and on target. You have felt awkward; and you have, it is hoped, felt completely yourself. You have comforted, and you received comfort. At times, you wondered where God was in all of this; and at other times, God's presence and love were so strong in your group that it took your breath away.

Now is the time for bringing your group's experience and life together to a close—for now. Reflect on your journey together and with Christ. Let's celebrate, encourage, and affirm. And let's give thanks.

Closing Prayer

10 minutes

Take turns thanking God for all the good things that have happened in your small group.

Read aloud the following verses from Philippians 1:3-11 (CEV) as a blessing for the group and dismissal:

> Every time I think of you, I thank my God. And whenever I mention you in my prayers, it makes me happy. This is because you have taken part with me in spreading the good news from the first day you heard about it. God is the one who began this good work in you, and I am certain that [God] won't stop before it is complete on the day that Christ Jesus returns.
>
> You have a special place in my heart. . . . [God] knows that I care for you in the same way that Christ Jesus does.
>
> I pray that your love will keep on growing and that you will fully know and understand how to make the right choices. Then you will still be pure and innocent when Christ returns. And until that day, Jesus Christ will keep you busy doing good deeds that bring glory and praise to God. Amen.

Hand each person his or her "Encouraging Words" paper as a keepsake.